CW01183752

Love's Unrelenting Course

Love's Unrelenting Course

One Woman's Secret Life of Bondage to
Sexual Trafficking and Abuse and How
She Found A Way Through to Freedom

Tom Steward

Copyright © 2021 by Tom Steward.

Library of Congress Control Number:		2021907217
ISBN:	Hardcover	978-1-6641-6754-4
	Softcover	978-1-6641-6753-7
	eBook	978-1-6641-6752-0

All rights reserved. No part of this book may be reproduced or transmitted in any form or by any means, electronic or mechanical, including photocopying, recording, or by any information storage and retrieval system, without permission in writing from the copyright owner.

Any people depicted in stock imagery provided by Getty Images are models, and such images are being used for illustrative purposes only. Certain stock imagery © Getty Images.

Print information available on the last page.

Rev. date: 04/26/2021

To order additional copies of this book, contact:
Xlibris
844-714-8691
www.Xlibris.com
Orders@Xlibris.com
804885

This book is dedicated to all women who live closeted lives because their abusers forbid them to speak the truth. For all of you women, even though you hide in secret, feeling afraid, ashamed, and that no one cares, you are seen. You are known. You are valued. You are so very loved beyond what you know. May you be given strength to come out of hiding at the right time so that you can live a life of freedom and fullness.

This book is also dedicated to all parents who have lost a child. Your precious son or daughter, as a child or an adult, has been taken from you, perhaps in the most painful way. Your heart aches with a stabbing pain and an emptiness that you may believe you could never recover from. May you be comforted knowing that there are others who share your pain and that your cherished child is now in a state of grace, love, and beauty. May you have glimpses of your beloved one on the other side of the veil and see them as their true eternal self in a way that provides significant comfort.

And finally, this book is dedicated to all children who have been forced to endure abuse from anyone in their lives. Your body and heart have been ravaged and treated without care because of someone else's cruelty. May you know release, freedom, and comfort some time very soon. May someone extend themselves into your life in order to demonstrate to you that you are prized and important, and may you find a way beyond the dreadful circumstances of your young years to become a strong and mature adult when that time comes.

This book is based on true and actual events. It is the story of the life of one particular woman. She has been a counseling client of mine, and she has granted me full permission to reveal the story of her life.

Names have been either withheld or changed to protect the identity of those involved.

This book is not meant to malign any individual or to suggest any criminal involvement. I hope that the story would speak for itself, and any indication of unlawful behavior would be processed by law enforcement through a criminal investigation as deemed necessary.

Law enforcement had been consulted on countless occasions regarding what is written here, and extensive reports had been filed in two separate counties in the state in which these actions occurred.

Incidentally, those who had committed the malicious acts that I have recorded in this book are now deceased. This is true in every case except one.

It is my hope that justice will be served and that perpetrators of any and all forms of exploitation everywhere will be held accountable for their actions. I also hope that all who have experienced harm and abuse would know freedom and release.

At our core, all humans are loving, full of love in their heart of hearts. To return to love the self and others so that this power from the Divine or the Source is evident in our lives is a worthy goal indeed.

May this writing achieve these purposes.

Contents

Foreword xi

1. Eternity's Light Cast on Winter's Soft Shadows 1
2. Being Who You Already Are 5
3. Thrown Headlong, Get Up Running 9
4. A Human for Sale 15
5. A Son Registered Only in Heaven 23
6. Freedom 31
7. Unholy Matrimony 38
8. Ambrosia's Subtle Soothing 53
9. Sexual Trafficking of Children in America 62
10. Healing the Brokenhearted 72
11. Much Love to You 82

Afterword 93

Foreword

Secrets

This writing is one that contains many secrets. These secrets have been held quietly in the safe trust of private lives, particularly of one. These secrets have been progressively released over a long season of trusting and telling. This writing is a further unveiling of dark secrets that at times seemed too astounding to be true. What is written here is nothing but the truth, so help me God.

This is the story of a particular woman whom I have known for several years now. What is written here is meant for the general public, to let anyone and everyone know what is really occurring behind a well-crafted presentation. If you would be given hope in the midst of any struggle you are going through, this revealing will be worth the effort.

What is interesting is that many of this woman's family and circle of friends and the wider community where she lives have no idea about the details written here. This will be new information for many, and it may very well be quite shocking. There may even be a sense of betrayal experienced. Some might ask, "How could she keep this from those closest to her?"

That her life had been a carefully crafted secret is a key part of the story. It may become clear as you read why she felt the need to not speak the truth of what her life had become. Fear is a predominant core state for humans, as well as shame. These inner states represent the sidewalls, decor, and furnishings of the interior house of the soul for each one of us to one degree or another. There are those who live by shame and fear more intensely than others.

Deception and Demolitions

Sir Walter Scott had written, "What a tangled web we weave when first we practice to deceive!" (1). As the weaving of the web begins, even by kind and normally honest individuals, its necessity builds, and the lie extends its insidious circumference. Lies build on lies because it is determined that the secrets are too unbearable to be exposed. Who would believe it? Shame and fear are the energies driving this force, and it takes a greater power to shatter this construction.

Rumi, the gifted Persian poet, offered long ago that "in this life many demolitions are actually renovations" (2). I know about this woman's demolitions. She let me in to observe the horror and agony of it all. I have also been a witness to the renovations as her life—piece by piece, thread by thread—was sewn back together into a garment of wholeness.

Kintsugi and Wabi-Sabi

Kintsugi is the centuries-old art of repairing broken pottery with gold. Kintsugi means "golden joinery" or "golden repair." Pottery that had been cracked or shattered can be remedied with a special lacquer dusted with powdered gold, silver, or platinum. Such exquisitely beautiful applications of gold are delicately brushed into the cracks of the ceramic ware, presenting a unique appearance to the reconstructed masterpiece.

"In offering this means of restoration, each artifact's unique history is celebrated by emphasizing its fractures and breaks instead of hiding or disguising them" (3). This practice coincides with the Japanese philosophy of *wabi-sabi*, which allows beauty to be seen in that which had been deemed flawed or imperfect. In this way, a piece of art becomes even more beautiful than it was prior to its breaking.

The practice of kintsugi is reflected in this woman's life. She was broken, and her fractured essence had been repaired by a golden adhesive as fragments of her shattered life were reformed to represent exquisite beauty. This, to me, is quite incredible, and it is why her story must be told.

1. Sir Walter Scott, Marmion: A Tale of Flodden Field, A Poem in Six Cantos
2. The Essential Rumi
3. https://mymodernmet.com/kintsugi-kintsukuroi

1
Eternity's Light Cast on Winter's Soft Shadows

Small Beginnings

When she first came to see me, it was in the long dark season of December's snowy winter. I guided her to my office, and she sat down on the couch. She was tentative and demure, and I detected a fear that seemed to cascade through her that was subtly palpable. Something like terror bled from her eyes as she sent out a nonverbal plea: "Help me!" Yet there was also a discernable hesitance as if she wasn't sure she could trust me. The development of trust would take its time as the weeks and months stretched into years.

Outside my office window, I noticed the snow begin to gently fall, and I directed her attention to this sight. We observed the snow's shimmering translucence that was flanked by the sky's black canvass. There was something special about this beginning that we could not fully perceive or appreciate at the time. I would come to find out later how important snowfall was to her. It has marked significant events in her life in which timely divine intervention was represented when it was needed the most.

I engaged her in conversation in this beginning encounter, yet her words were few. It was obvious that she was in pain—physically, emotionally, and otherwise—yet it was not initially clear why. I would come to find over the protracted course ahead that she had ample reason to harbor the flickering psychic states of fear and pain.

She had a story, one of the most tragic accounts of abuse and violation of body and soul that I have ever heard. All of this was securely hidden beneath the draped-over veneer of a pastor's wife in a Christian community.

For a long time, so very long, I was the only person (other than her abusers) who knew the secrets she had kept hidden for decades. How could she have endured this alone for so long? It must have been a heavy, unbearable weight. I was more than willing to shoulder some of the burden for her. If only I could carry more.

"Misty Water-Colored Memories"

She had memories, intense images, of a lifetime of abuse marking the landscape of her interior topography, yet I had no idea at this point to what extent. During this first session, she began to tell me some of what she had been through.

As a psychotherapist, I moved into my favorite therapeutic tool when I hear of trauma. I engaged her in EMDR—Eye Movement Desensitization and Reprocessing—yet the usual outcome did not occur. This was because of blindness in one of her eyes, which made it impossible for her eyes to maintain the required bilateral motion necessary for this technique.

I had to find a way to cut off the rough edges of her traumatic experiences and smooth out her response to her unbearable history, yet the first step was for her to tell me about these details.

I spent the rest of our time at this first meeting listening to whatever limited version of her story she was willing to provide. I knew I needed to be gentle and patient so that she would come to trust me and this process.

Manageable Disclosure

She left the meeting hardly any better because of the tentativeness that put her on edge and unable to ingest any level of kindness I sought to offer. She was still trying to discern if I could be trusted. As I walked her to the door, I wondered what was trapped inside of her and if I had any chance to help her unload the heavy yoke around her neck that years of turmoil and disappointment left her with.

Her husband would greet her in the parking lot before each of our meetings, at least for the first year or two of counseling. He would also wait for her after each session. Early on, there was one time that he came up to meet me, presumably to scope me out and make sure I did not present any danger to their secret life. He needed to make sure her conversations with me were limited because he didn't want her to tell me anything that would jeopardize him.

There was only so much she was allowed to say to me because he demanded a detailed account from her regarding what occurred in our sessions. He needed to control her therapy and everything else about her life, for that matter. He had a lot to hide, as I would come to find.

After we had met a few times, he asked her, "When is he going to fix you?" His goal was for this therapy to be short lived and to dispatch of it as soon as possible. Her talking to me was a threat to him and the diabolical world he had created for her. He wanted to be certain that what they were living remained their tainted little secret that no one else would be privy to.

During each of our sessions together, she would gingerly and carefully unravel the contents of her life. There was a tension between what she longed to tell me and what she was told to reveal. She had been crouched behind a veil of deception not only because her husband didn't want her to expose him but also because she didn't want to be reminded of the anguishing specifics of her burdensome life. She was so ashamed of what her life had become in every aspect.

It became apparent in our conversations that I needed to ask specific questions or she wouldn't provide details. If I asked vague or general questions, I would receive vague or general answers. If I didn't ask open-ended questions, she would provide only a short monosyllabic response. She taught me to be specific, especially with her. As I sharpened my skill of asking pertinent and precise questions, I received the answers that would allow me to put the puzzle pieces together of her tormented existence. Yet this would take a considerable amount of time.

Writing Out Her Story

Since she had so much difficulty speaking about her story for multiple reasons, I suggested she record the contents of her life and provide me with the typed document. She did this for a while, and I have a folder full of her life experiences.

In this folder are the following notes she wrote to me: "Wow, what a whirlwind of a ride. Never thought I would ever share as much as I have with you . . . I have not felt safe enough to share until now, so thank you. Took me long enough to gain trust to share. This is extremely hard for me."

And also, "Thank you for not judging me . . . You showed me compassion without judgment. Thank you," and, "You kept your word and allowed me to share in a safe place and did not judge me or condemn me, which was huge for me. Right there you gained my trust . . . So, that means I am now able to share with you some other things I hold VERY close to my heart, in hopes that I am safe sharing these as well."

In the following note she also accounted for the memories that began to surface during the first few months of therapy. "Memories . . . I am really disliking memories." And also: "I cannot get over the memories. And the smell in each one, why I remember that is beyond me . . . I don't want to remember them anymore. I want them to go away. And it's like it's unlocking more and more memories I had totally forgotten."

And then there were her nightmares at night and her flashbacks during the day: "The nightmares are not only getting old, they are beginning to make me angry." Additionally, "I can't seem to get those horrific and graphic scenes out of my mind. They just won't go away. Up until now they have pretty much just shown back up through nightmares, but now I am having flashbacks during the day."

This is the story of this woman's life that she has allowed me the honor to tell, bittersweet as it is. What I have heard has broken my heart over and over again. This woman and I hope that this will benefit someone, perhaps even many.

2
Being Who You Already Are

Transcendence

Here we are in my office many years after I first met her. This woman is sitting before me strong and at peace. I never thought this would be possible for her, yet something grand and mysterious has opened up and captured us willingly.

In the beginning, the trajectory toward even the smallest amount of progress seemed long and impossible. Yet, in due time, great things did occur. I now know that anything is possible and that a miracle in life is within grasp for every one of us.

The path to this heightened state of growth has been remarkable. She is now resolute and determined, confident in her identity—who she is—and her purpose—why she is here.

Free at Last

She is free. She spoke to me so many times during this entire process about her wish for freedom. I can say now, decidedly and unequivocally, that she knows freedom, as much as it is possible at the present time.

She wanted nothing more than her own release, and she has now come into this place after many years of imprisonment. I often thought of her as a weak, defenseless bird in a cage, trapped behind an enclosure; even as it opened, she did not possess the awareness or resolve to retreat into the safety that she so longed for.

Our perceived enclosures are often imagined more than they are real. Freedom is understood to be beyond our grasp but only because we believe it to be. What we refer to as our reality is concocted; we made it all up, most often toward detrimental conclusions.

What we believe becomes our reality, despite any attempt from our self or others to convince us otherwise. This is because "we don't see things as they are, we see them as we are" (1). What we see is the only reality we know although there is a vast world about us that could help us draw better conclusions, which we unilaterally ignore on a consistent basis.

Yet for this woman there are now only a few lasting effects from the consciousness of the entrapment that once defined her life. It is said of Christ that his primary purpose in coming to earth was to heal the brokenhearted, to release the captives, and to set the prisoners free (2). One translator of this text from the original language of Greek offered that the great teacher came to "release those who are broken by calamity" (3).

This woman has been released from calamity's shattering. She is not only out of her containment, but she flies. There are times she soars, gliding in the current of the prevailing wind that enables her to rise above and transcend everything she has experienced in any previous time.

Truth in the Innermost Being

This woman is, by natural inclination, honest. This is the case, at least on the surface, yet the deception she had to live by went against her very nature. She knew that to lie was essential or someone would find out, and they would know of her shame-saturated weakness. They would discover that she failed to protect herself as if there was something wrong with her because she played a role in creating this nightmare of a life. The vast chasm between the life she was living and the one she was projecting through her social facade was apparently too far apart to be reconciled.

She had to protect her abusers, yet she also had to protect herself, mostly her own decimated heart. This was her time-torn heart center that was ravaged by long years of pummeling and pounding.

For so long she didn't believe anyone would accept her for who she really was and what she had been through. Who would believe this story or even provide support, especially in the Christian community where everyone appeared to be exhibiting their glittering images?

Yet all she wanted was to find a way to exit her dungeon of despair. And now, she has finally solved the puzzle of Ariadne's thread, and she has been released from her maze of torment. She has bridged the gap of this gulf between what is presented as her social self and what is lived behind the walls of her previously fabricated facade.

She is true to herself and others. She is honest, not willing to cower behind any manufactured cardboard cover. She is open as she offers herself and her truth, the real truth of who she is, to all who come into contact with her.

There is now hardly any pretense in her at all, only the genuine heartfelt true nature that reflects divinity to her core. Those who know her are able to experience a sincere, purposeful intention to be honest and real. And this, she is.

Strong Love

She has always been kind, often to a fault, providing more for others than she was intended to give. She concluded that love was defined by endless giving. Whatever the other person wanted, she offered.

She found, through the pain of it all, that this is not true love mostly because it depletes the inner core and devalues the self. For love to be true, she has realized that she needs to give it to herself first. Her love for herself is evidenced in a quiet devotion to her own best interests as she nurtures her contact with the author of love who is love itself. It is this source of love who proclaimed that we are to love ourselves first and then love others. The order and direction for this love is pertinent (4).

She is now a strong dispenser of healthy love. She would and can do most anything for anyone, yet this does not deplete her. The love that she has found actually grows in its expression. It is a presentation that pays incessant dividends. The compassionate kindness born in true love is so potent that it finds its target every time and also expands on release.

Physical Healing

There is something else that is very interesting, even miraculous. The physical tension and fear-based anxiety she knew through the years have been significantly diminished. This is because she has traveled a long way to resolve the stubborn core state of fear that plagued her for so long. She is fierce, fearless, and with unabashed courage. How this stands in contrast to what I saw when I first met her is remarkable.

She has always been racked by physical pain as all of her bones and joints and muscles scream in unending agony. I have seen her bend in pain from her lower back as she waddled across the room. I have observed her wince as she attempted to sit down or get out of a chair because of the pain in various parts of her body. She still has her physical pain but not nearly as much as before.

I suppose it is quite true that we store our emotional, psychological, and spiritual issues in our physical frame. If this is so, then receiving any measure of healing in each of these areas will heal the physical body as well. It's as if the physical body regenerates in response to emotional well-being. That this occurs without any direct attention to the body is a welcome gift.

I could go on, but I believe you get the idea. I would like to tell you now how it all began. It is my aim to reveal to you her early life and its progression through the long and battle-scarred years that culminated in a life of tragedy.

Now that you know there is a positive end, I hope you will be intrigued to read this story that shifts gracefully into hope that will lift any heart.

1. Anaïs Nin
2. Luke 4:18
3. Kenneth S. Wuest, The New Testament: An Expanded Translation
4. Matthew 22:39

3
Thrown Headlong, Get Up Running

Early Years

She was born on a snowy afternoon in Laramie, Wyoming, in 1969. Her grandparents owned a cattle ranch in Northern Colorado along the Laramie River, bordering the Rawah wilderness. The ranch was two hours north of Fort Collins, Colorado, and an hour and forty-five minutes south of Laramie, Wyoming.

Her family, along with her grandparents, aunt, uncle, and cousins, all lived on the ranch. Every family had their separate home, and her house was a part of the main building on the upper ranch. Her cousins, along with their parents—her aunt and uncle—lived in a house on the lower ranch. She loved growing up with her cousins and her older sister. The ranch was a zone of safety and adventure.

She suffered from multiple medical complications for most of her childhood. She was diagnosed early in life with childhood asthma. Her asthma was so severe that she couldn't run across the living room without passing out. She carried around a brown paper bag everywhere she went in case she developed an asthma attack.

She was diagnosed with hypothyroidism at one and a half years old and juvenile arthritis in elementary school. She had high fevers for long periods of time, which caused permanent hearing loss in one ear and loss of sight in one eye. Both these issues with her sight and hearing were determined to be irreparable, and she endures these limitations to this day.

Since childhood, she had been unable to control her body temperature. She could become overheated or really cold very easily. Because of the weakness of her body and immune system, she had many infections, including countless bouts with pneumonia, strep, and bronchitis.

She had allergies to nearly everything, especially chemicals. She was not able to take medications because of severe allergic reactions. For a while she was given additional medications to counteract these detrimental effects, which made her even more ill. She even hallucinated on numerous occasions because of an adverse reaction to medications.

She spent a lot of her early years in the hospital in Fort Collins. From her recollection it seemed as if she was in the hospital more than she was at home. She remembers many days in the hospital playing games with the nurses. Much of her memories are about being with nurses, and she does not recall as many instances of her parents being present.

She does have more memories of her father being present in the hospital. Her father, who is now deceased, told her stories of the difficult times at the ranch with her health issues. There were countless times he would wake up in the middle of the night and she would not be breathing. They would then travel to the hospital in Fort Collins. En route, her father would hold her upright in his lap all the way to the emergency room, hoping she would continue breathing until they secured medical help. She would remain in the hospital, and her father would stay for as long as he could until he had to go back to work or to college, or to the ranch.

Doctors told her parents that she would not survive past the age of seven, if that long. Her mother took her off all her medications when she was seven because she didn't want to play nursemaid anymore. Her mother told God to either heal her or end her life. Her mother was willing for her daughter to die because she was so overwhelmed with having a constantly ill child. This woman, however, remembers very little of her mother playing any nurturing role over those very difficult years.

Reflecting on her childhood and the parenting she received, she knows her parents were very troubled. Their marriage was often in jeopardy, and they did eventually divorce. She remembers her mom being mentally and verbally abusive, and very impatient with her illnesses. Her dad was physically abusive to her and had a temper that flared up easily, often because of her mother.

Their care of her during her frequent illnesses and medical crises must have been existent. She does know, however, that she did not receive the kind of loving care a young child needs, especially when there is such a significant amount of medical trauma. Those years must have been very challenging for everyone.

Even in the context of those difficult days, she does realize that her father loved her. She knows he did a lot for her. Her mother must have loved her in her own way. She felt, however, as if there was something lacking. She developed a hole in her heart that would stay with her for many years. As she grew older, something in her caused her to look all around for love and acceptance, ostensibly because this was missing in her formative years.

Snowfall

Her parents decided at one point to move to Fort Collins to be closer to the doctors and the hospital. She was still able to spend weekends and summers at the ranch, and she enjoyed these times immensely. At the ranch, however, she was frequently confined to her bed. She remembers looking out the window of her room to see her sister and cousins playing in the snow. She was so jealous that she would sneak out to play with them.

She would stand outside in the snowfall, catching snowflakes on her eye lashes and hands. She developed a love for snow and each plunging snowflake, appreciating the beauty of this miracle from heaven. Each snowflake falling from the open sky was so unique and very fragile. She observed each plummeting snowflake that descended from above, noting them to have a gentle and subtle power.

Her experience with snowfall even as a child was that they would create a blanket of peace over the world. This would allow her to admire in silence this presentation of wonder. Her perspective as a little girl was that even her parents would stop fighting when it was snowing.

She cherished these treasured moments with snow between the many moments of being sick and confined to her bed or going to the hospital for long stretches. Throughout all of the crises and trying moments in her life, every one of them is occasioned by the gift of falling snow.

"Brain Damage"

She moved to our town in Northern New Mexico in the winter of 1978 while she was in the fourth grade. Her father was able to secure a job at the scientific laboratory in town.

Either because of the course of her medical treatment or the medications that she was given at such a young age, she developed what she referred to as "brain damage." She was also kicked in the head by a horse, which didn't help. She spoke of processing errors, which forced her to take more time to understand information that others were able to gather much more quickly.

She also had memory retention issues and difficulty recalling even the smallest items. She told me that she typically had to read something several times and draw visual pictures to help her process information. She did receive assistance and was in the special education program from elementary through twelfth grade of high school.

During one of our sessions, I began to speak with her about the VAK. This was a tool I learned many years ago when I was trained in Psych-K, developed by Rob Williams. Psych-K is based on the work of Bruce Lipton, a cellular biologist who taught medical students at Stanford. Lipton wrote the book *The Biology of Belief,* which is a groundbreaking offering that revealed how our cells receive and process information. What Dr. Lipton found in his research paved the way for Williams to develop Psych-K.

Psych-K is an energy psychology tool that elicits embedded subconscious beliefs and clears them. The VAK integrates new thoughts and beliefs in order to assimilate them from the deep unconscious into the conscious mind. The "V" stands for visual, the "A" is for auditory, and the "K" is for kinesthetic. This accounts for how we learn new material in order to integrate this information into long-term memory. We have to see it in action in our lives: *visual.* We need to hear ourselves and others commenting about it: *auditory.* We then feel it kinesthetically in the body: *kinesthetic.* Williams called this tool "VAK to the Future."

As I was explaining the VAK to this woman on one particular session, she proclaimed that it was what she has been doing since childhood in order to learn new information. I was stunned. Somehow, even as a young child she had known she had trouble learning, which impacted her school experience. Yet she also knew she had to learn, and in her tenacity she developed a strategy in order to get the most out of her education.

What she developed as a child was roughly similar to what a licensed psychotherapist also developed based on groundbreaking scientific research, made into a learning tool that has crossed the globe many times over. Amazing!

The Accident

When she was in the sixth grade, she was in the downtown area of our small town and her mother picked her and her sister up. They had plans to go out and eat lunch with their father. She recalls that this didn't happen very often, but there was something they had to deal with as a family.

They couldn't find her father, so her mom parked in front of the post office. Her mother asked her to run across the street to the local department store to use the phone and call her dad. So she ventured across the street to speak with her father by phone to confirm their plans to meet. She then had every intention to walk back across the street to let her mom know what her dad said.

Since it was lunchtime and also a payday for those who worked at the laboratory, there was a lot of traffic on the small downtown street. The eastbound traffic stopped for her to cross. She looked to the right and didn't see any cars although the sun was bright, which obscured her vision. As she stepped out into the crosswalk she looked again just as a car hit her. She said that the car hit her so hard she was thrown headlong to the ground, flipping her at least six feet in the air.

There was an off-duty police officer who just happened to be standing on the corner of the street and saw everything unfold. The officer reported later that she landed on her head and had toppled over several times for a considerable distance. He also related that the driver was going over forty-five miles an hour, which was almost twice the speed limit in that stretch of the downtown area. The driver later claimed he never saw her, which was most likely because of the glaring sun that affected his vision as well.

She suffered a concussion, a fractured cheekbone, and injuries to her neck. She had bruises all over her body, with flesh removed to the bone on her elbows, knees, and one of her hips.

After she landed and was sprawled out on the street, people came over to help her. She immediately became frightened and bewildered, not comfortable with that measure of attention. Disregarding her injuries and need for medical care, she sprang up and started running. The officer ran after her. He chased after her and made her lie down on the sidewalk while waiting for the ambulance. Medical personnel who arrived at the scene assessed her and decided to transport her to the hospital, but she didn't want to go. She was told that they would let her turn on the sirens, so she agreed to be transferred to the hospital in the ambulance. She was examined and attended to at the hospital and eventually released.

That was a Friday; she returned to school that next Monday. She remembers being in significant pain over that weekend and into the next week and beyond. That Monday the teacher had her stand up in front and tell the entire class what had happened. This was all to presumably stress the importance of crosswalk safety, looking both ways, and being careful while crossing the street. She related that this was so humiliating and that she felt like being made a spectacle of.

This chapter is entitled "Thrown Headlong, Get Up Running." Now you know why. This is the story of this woman's life. Every time she was tossed by the painful events of her life, she just kept getting up. Sometimes she even ran away from harm or potential danger.

She doesn't really like to focus on the pain of her life, so she had a habitual pattern of running away from it. At times, she didn't run because she couldn't. She was trapped. Yet in most circumstances she was able to get up and run away as quickly as possible. Where she was running to, even she didn't always know.

As for the many circumstances of her life, how she had been thrown headlong and how she had chosen to run away will become even clearer in the coming chapters.

4
A Human for Sale

A Mere Child

The fall of 1982 began like many others. The weather was unusually warm with no precipitation until the blustery months of winter arrived.

This was the beginning of her eighth grade. She started the school year like any other and not unlike how many young girls would. She was hopeful for what the new year would bring. Unbeknownst to her, in those beginning moments of the new school year she would engage on a trajectory that would change her life forever. She would be drawn into making choices that would alter the course of her life and take decades to recover from.

She was just a young girl, yet in her longing for acceptance, she looked around for whatever was available. A friend of hers invited her to parties, and she was eager to participate in those opportunities. She went to parties that were full of fun, alcohol, and whatever else was available to quell teenage angst and rebel against parental authority. Perhaps she could also receive the acceptance and validation she longed for.

At one of those parties, she was introduced to a young man who was friends with another man named Jimmy. Her conversation with Jimmy was initiated, and she later met his brother Marcos. These men would be responsible for tarnishing and ravaging her life in a way that was nothing short of diabolical.

The man, Jimmy, was in his early or mid-twenties, perhaps older. He began to seduce her. He spoke to her using all the right words to coax her in. They were the words of encouragement and acceptance that she needed to hear and was not receiving at home.

There was a gaping hole in her soul, and in her preadolescent longing she looked for someone or something to fill it. And even though she was only thirteen years old, still almost half a year away from her fourteenth birthday, Jimmy initiated a sexual relationship with her. As a young girl, she gave herself to him. The gap in their ages was more than ten years, yet no one seemed to notice or care.

He used words meant to appease her and to draw her in. Jimmy told her she was the best sexual partner he had ever had. He told her he wanted to teach her things about sex and life and help her in any way she needed.

The Introduction

He then told her about a man whom he was struggling with. Jimmy didn't know how to help that man and was perplexed about what to do, or so he said. He began to string a story about his need to provide something for that man and only she could help him with it. Words were used that included gentle pleading and kind persuasion.

Jimmy suggested that it might help if she were to go out to dinner with the man. She obeyed his request. She went out to dinner with the man, which seemed odd to her. She wasn't certain what she was supposed to do. The dinner date ended and that was that, until Jimmy wanted it to happen again.

His words were persuasive, not forceful yet persistent. He spoke in a way that influenced her to go out on another dinner date with that man. The two men were up to something that she was not able to discern at the time. They went out on a second dinner date, and this time it ended in sex. As a child she had sexual intercourse with a man in his forties.

Sold into Sexual Slavery

Looking back on it now, she knows Jimmy was grooming her for a role. He would tell her she was perfect and pure, and that he wanted to train her and mold her for something really important. He used all the right words, and as a young girl she was led into something slowly and convincingly, gradually becoming more and more impossible to retreat from.

His words were as slick as a salesman's, promising something more alluring than what he could provide. Reflecting on this time, she once told me, "I just wanted to be important and loved." She was not able to distinguish deception from truth because, sadly, she did not know true love from its counterfeit. Someone saw her weakness and was cruel enough to use her in a way that began to destroy her soul. Jimmy had only one intention, which was to manipulate her for his purposes.

She thought she was gaining acceptance and validation, but she was actually being primed for sexual slavery. She could have run; she didn't have to consent, yet the shameless deception offered to her made her participation believable and harmless.

Jimmy said she was his prize, so special that he was willing to share her with others. She felt degraded as if she was doing something wrong, and the more she proceeded, the more trapped she felt.

Jimmy set up more meetings with other men. Soon she was with countless men each week. Jimmy would find the men, and he would arrange for her to have sex with them. He would receive payment in cash or drugs, yet he never gave any of the proceeds to her. Never! He took all of the money and provided no compensation for her life of prostitution because he told her it was a privilege for her to be in his service.

Then Jimmy's attitude and demeanor began to change. He became sullen and cross, and would become angry with her more frequently and demand more of her. It happened most often whenever there was any hint of her resisting from doing what he wanted. This was swiftly met with his rage as he became more and more forceful with her.

Her significant health issues were still present and remained a concern, yet no one cared about her physical health let alone her emotional well-being. Even more, what was occurring in her life made her sick to her stomach. Her body often ached with what she was asked to do, and her little girl heart became ravaged as each day pressed forward.

Marcos, Jimmy's younger brother, started getting jealous of her time with Jimmy. Jimmy claimed her as his own and used her for business as well as his personal sexual partner. This infuriated Marcos. Marcos started to follow her around, stalking her because he wanted something for himself in spite of his brother. Even though Jimmy forbade Marcos to go anywhere near her, Marcos stealthily gained access to her. It was at this time that Marcos began to rape her on a weekly basis.

She decided to tell Jimmy about what his brother was doing to her. When she did, he smacked her on the face and told her to never talk about Marcos that way again. She suddenly realized that she was being used and abused on many fronts and no one was present to protect her or defend her. She was alone and trapped in something she had no idea how to retreat from.

On the Edge of Oblivion

During this entire ordeal, she was remarkably compliant. There was only one time when she wasn't. Jimmy connected her with a man that she was expected to have sex with. The man was old, smelly, and gross, and she just couldn't follow through with what was demanded of her. She became so nauseated that she thought she might vomit. She let the man know this and left.

Jimmy, of course, found out and decided to talk to her about it. He seemed calm as he let her tell her version of the story. Then he took her for a drive presumably just to talk.

Jimmy drove through the streets of our mountain town. The town was anywhere from 7,000 to 7,500 feet high. There was one particular road that ascended up to the town's ski hill. The base of the ski hill at the lodge was 9,200 feet, and the elevation reaches 10,400 feet at the top of the ski runs. The town was situated among flat top mesas and canyons with steep precipitous slopes.

Jimmy drove on the meandering road up the mountain toward the ski hill and stopped on the side of the road. He parked and invited her out of the car. They stood on a cliff edge overlooking a canyon. He spoke with such nonchalance that she thought nothing was amiss. The scenery was picturesque with the mountains nearby and the sight below featuring our famed town.

She concluded that Jimmy was not as upset as she thought he would be. Then the conversation turned, and Jimmy made an ominous comment.

His exact words were, "What you did last night destroyed me, and now I am going to do to you what you did to me." He then took her by the throat and, with her back to the cliff edge, pushed her backwards over the steep slope with the aim of ending her life.

She fell—or more accurately, rolled—down the side of the cliff very precipitously in a death-defying freefall. The cliff was not so steep that it led straight down, but it was steep enough that she could not control her descent. In recalling the event with me once, she told me that there was no way she could stop herself from falling. By the time she reached the bottom, possibly five hundred to six hundred feet down the slope, she realized her injuries were significant.

After some time, she was somehow able to walk, cautiously and in great pain, through the forest. She was able to find the road and began her trek toward town. An old man in an old beaten pick-up saw her and stopped. He asked her if she was all right, and she gave him a scant version of the truth. He must have sensed her need for help, so he drove her into town and to the hospital. In pain, she lifted herself out of the truck, but she never went into the hospital and no one else found out about the incident. She has injuries from that fall that to this day have never fully healed.

A Cliffside Revisit

A few years ago, I returned to the side of this cliff with her. We looked down in shocked amazement that she had survived that plummet. I observed the site, trying to imagine what it would have been like for her as a young girl to roll as dangerously and rapidly as she did.

I then tried to envision what it was like for her to sit at the bottom of the cliff and survey the damages to her body. She must have wondered how she could get back to some safe reprieve, or if there was any way to get help. She may have pondered how she managed to still be alive.

It certainly wasn't Jimmy's objective for her to live. He wanted to kill her. If she was going to resist his orders, he had no use for her.

As we stared down the slope that was the location of one of the most frightening events of her life, she seemed visibly shaken and overwhelmed with emotion. I comforted her, providing her with the compassion and connection that she had needed then but did not receive.

She did recall that as she was descending down the cliff, her descent was halted by an object, perhaps a tree or a rock. She was convinced that if that did not happen, she would most assuredly have died.

Following this brush with death, she returned to her role in the business. You may be thinking that this could have been an opportunity for her to escape. But she was so hooked by then and was also deeply fearful for her life that she surmised her only option was to surrender again to the madness of what her life had become.

After being thrown off the cliff, her perspective started to change. It was at this time that she began to make plans for her escape. This needed to be held secretly within her or her plot would certainly be found out.

Pregnancy, Marriage, Death, and Other Small-Town Adventures

When she was fifteen years old, she became pregnant. The father? It was Marcos. Consequently, Jimmy couldn't sell her while she was pregnant, so she was out of commission for a while. She once told me that because of the pregnancy she went from being a valued commodity to being used goods and was suddenly expendable.

In another sadistic turn of events, she married Jimmy. Jimmy was angry at her for becoming pregnant as if it was her fault. She knew very clearly that he wanted to get rid of the child. I am guessing Jimmy married her to get closer because he had plans to kill her baby. It was a prostitution business, not a nursery for valued children.

The marriage occurred in the summer of 1985, just two months after her giving birth. She was impregnated by one brother, married to the other, and a sexual slave to many. It does not go unnoticed that all of these were criminal acts inflicted on a minor child.

Of all places, the marriage ceremony occurred at our local cemetery, on the green grass above the deceased who were marked by headstones for remembrance. She described the ceremony as something like a satanic ritual officiated by none other than the jealous younger brother, Marcos.

It was, of course, a sham marriage with no certificate sanctioned by local authorities.

Then, in the fall of 1985, something happened. Jimmy and Marcos were racing on a freeway in California, and Marcos used his vehicle to push Jimmy's car off the road. The vehicle flipped numerous times, and Jimmy was killed. Her so-called marriage to Jimmy ended after a few months.

So now Marcos had her all to himself, and he became chief operator of the family prostitution business. Once he returned, he also blamed her for killing Jimmy. According to Marcos, his brother's death was all her fault. Through his degrading words, it was obvious that he was poised to seek vengeance for his brother's death. He even said, "You're going to pay for this."

A Town of Historic Significance

We live in a relatively small city of about eighteen thousand people. You most likely know of this town. There is a scientific laboratory here that is responsible for developing the atomic bomb that brought World War II to an abrupt halt.

This is the town that has been known as the secret city with a clandestine government operation in the 1940s known as the Manhattan Project. Over time and through the decades since the second world war, this town has expanded its operations into other notable scientific endeavors. We don't just build bombs here. We are engaged in cutting-edge science that is changing the world.

During the early to mid-1980s, many of this woman's clients whom she was forced to have sex with were employees of the laboratory. What is even more disconcerting is that many of these transactions involved drugs. That there were government employees rampantly engaged in illegal sexual behavior with a minor and that illicit drugs were involved is certainly a matter of national security.

All Across America

I once asked her if there were other young girls involved in the business of sexual slavery in our town, and she said yes. She knew of a few others, one in particular named Allison. Allison will play a role in her life in the next chapter, so keep her in mind.

What can be revealed about Allison here is that at one point, she suddenly disappeared. This woman had always presumed that Allison was killed because she, too, wanted out. She knows this because she spoke with Allison about her plans to escape.

I once asked this woman another question. Did she think this version of prostitution was still going on now? She said it was most likely still occurring. Sexual trafficking happens in towns, small and large and in between, all across America as we live under the delusion that we are the greatest country on the earth, the land of the free and home of the brave.

You are only as strong as your weakest link. You cannot be great if there are those who are victimized in a culture that is willing to either bring harm or look away, pretending it doesn't exist.

Children in America are being prostituted. The young in our culture are violated against their will in the most egregious ways. Underage females, young women, and little girls are the commodity for yet another version of American slavery. The innocents are forced into something they are not complicit with. Young boys are also victimized in this manner, in ways that most do not know about.

This is a horrible reality. It is definitely occurring much more frequently than any of us would like to admit.

5
A Son Registered Only in Heaven

Shotgun Delivery with a Whiskey Chaser

On the evening of April 26, 1985, she gave birth to a baby boy in her family home. She named him Timothy Dean Colt and called him Timmy.

She made that name up herself. She always liked Timothy, which to her meant strength. She had a friend in high school named Dean who had a strong character, so she added that as a middle name. She always had a fascination with guns, so . . . Colt, as in the revolver.

During her pregnancy, she consulted with a public health nurse at the hospital. She did this to gain pointers on how to deliver a baby. The health nurse provided her with a syringe to clear the baby's lungs and nose. She got vice grips to pinch the umbilical cord and a knife to cut it. She also secured a towel to wrap the newborn.

That nurse had a hunch that she would be delivering the baby herself. She did not want to go to the hospital in the fear that her unlawful life and its product, the child, would be discovered. There also wasn't anyone else around who wanted to help her, so she needed to do it all by herself. Or maybe it was her shame that made her not want to receive help or let anyone know what her life had become.

She doesn't remember anyone in her family being around that entire weekend. Her father was presumably on travel, and she didn't know where her mother was. She does not recall seeing her at all. Her sister had already moved out by then. She once told me, "I was there by myself, sitting in the bathtub, with a bottle of whiskey in one hand and a shotgun in the other."

The shotgun was in case Marcos came by. He knew that at some point she would be delivering the baby, whom he didn't want to live.

Playing the role of an ob-gyn with a minimum supply of equipment and knowledge, she delivered a baby boy. She remarked to me once, "He was teeny tiny." She guessed he was barely five pounds.

She once wrote to me about her pregnancy:

> "The pregnancy went very well. I didn't have any morning sickness. In fact, I didn't even realize I was pregnant until I was almost three months along. I loved being pregnant and was so excited to be a mom. I was also terrified of being a teenage mom. I remember gaining maybe fifteen pounds during the entire pregnancy, and I barely showed. He (Timmy) came a few weeks early. About a week before Timmy was born, I met with my friend who was a nurse at public health. She said it would be ideal to go into the hospital for the delivery, but knowing me as she did, she gave me instructions on how to give birth at home. I am so thankful she did. It was late on a Friday evening, my dad was on travel and more than likely my mom was too, and (her sister) had already moved out. I was home alone. I got everything that I needed ready. When it got close, I drew a shallow warm bath and finished the delivery in the tub. The whiskey was helping with the pain, but . . . Um . . . not really. I think it gave me more courage than anything. At one point after his head was out, I remember feeling his shoulder come out. As painful as this was without meds, I was thrilled to be able to feel every part of him emerge. Wow! After his birth I got him cleaned out and cleaned up, and myself. I documented what I could, then sat and held him for the rest of the night, in total amazement of what I had just been a part of. A beautiful miracle in my arms."

She went into public health the next morning for an examination. Everything turned out well, and her body was in fine shape following the delivery of a baby on her own. There was no birth certificate because Timmy was born at home with no medical attention provided. She did receive paperwork for a birth certificate from the health nurse, but she never turned it in.

I once asked her to tell me about her son, Timmy. She wrote this:

> "He was so amazing. He developed into a strong and handsome little boy. His smile would melt any grown adult and his eyes were stunning. He was built like a little linebacker and waddled like one too. When he took off, he went with confidence as if he was out to conquer the world. I would love to see him today. He was very strong-willed, but very sweet tempered. Never fussed or threw a fit. He knew what he wanted, but also knew I was mom. I had to be strict with him because of our situation, and somehow, he knew that. His giggle was hilarious. I would smile just looking at him. I miss him so much!"

A Bittersweet Return

The twenty-sixth, the day of Timmy's birth, was a Friday. Being as dutiful as she was, always following through on her commitments, she went back to school the next Monday morning. Keep in mind, she was sixteen—just sixteen years old! Not an occurrence most sixteen-year-olds could say they have marched through so gallantly.

She was able to continue the demands of high school responsibly with a baby because she had friends to help her watch Timmy when they were free from classes. He was passed around from friend to friend. Allison, whom I mentioned previously, watched him primarily as she was more available.

She had a little boy, but in due time she returned to prostitution. She was, however, no longer used as frequently. Her return wasn't out of choice; she was trapped. Marcos had a hold on her, and she was fearful for her life and the life of her son. Better the devil you know than the devil you don't know.

It was at this time that Marcos may have sensed he was losing his grip on her, so he clamped down harder. She had to adhere to his whims and demands because she was paranoid and fearful that Marcos would find her and do something to her and/or Timmy. She lived a life in fear, anticipating the worst that could happen. This was no strange fantasy. Marcos was capable of murder. He had already killed his brother.

Then the worst that could happen did happen.

The Murder and Burial of Innocence

On October 31, 1986, while in Allison's care, her precious son Timmy was stolen by Marcos. On November 1, the following day, Timmy was delivered back to his mother by the merciless father. He was chopped up and burned, and the pieces of his little body were returned to her in a wooden box. She could barely make out his face, yet she knew it was him.

She once wrote to me: "I listened to Marcos tell me what he did to Timmy in grave detail, but I prayed it wasn't true. When I opened the box, I realized it was all true."

When Marcos returned Timmy to her, he gave her a thorough account of how he killed her little baby boy. She is haunted to this day by this description. She has told no one about the details of the murder of an innocent child. This is information I do not know about and have not asked, therefore, I cannot and would not write about it here. All that needs to be said is that her dear son was savagely and ruthlessly murdered.

She took the box with her beautiful boy to a trail near the cemetery in our town. She hiked up through the forest to the side of a hill and found a spot that was perfect for her intentions. From where she was perched on the hillside, she was able to look directly toward the cemetery.

The particular place that she chose was in view of the children's cemetery where children were buried. This is the place where many parents have placed the remains of their children of varying ages over the years. What is remarkable was that from where she settled herself on the hillside, a clearing in the trees pointed directly to where other children have been laid to rest. It was as if there was a pre-designed opening in the forest just for her to lay her child on, in full view of other children who left the earth all too soon. She knew it was where Timmy needed to be.

She then prepared to bury her son within sight of all other deceased children. She wanted her son to be a full participant in this life, but sadly, he was not. She wanted him to be a full participant in death, but sadly, this did not appear to be the case either. The closest she could get Timmy to the other children who have passed on was that location on the hill side.

With a bottle of whiskey, a shot gun, and a shovel, she faced the task before her. She grabbed her shovel and dug a hole. With great sadness and a lot of tears, she positioned the box with her son into the ground. Then she shoveled the dirt over his physical remains. She sat down and began to sip from the whiskey bottle to soothe her tormenting grief and sorrow. Her baby was now laid to rest in the ground before her. She consumed the entire bottle in an attempt to deal with it all.

And then something incredible occurred. It was a miracle, a touch from God. It started snowing! And just like when she was a little girl, she looked up to observe as the beautiful snowflakes with their luminous effect as they fell ever so gently. She watched as beauty and wonder unfolded before her, and her heart was warmed.

She was also drunk, but never mind that. God can influence us by providing an intervention on his conditions without being influenced by our condition, even when we are under the influence. This is nothing less than sweet and timely *grace*.

Return to the Site

And that was that. She never returned to that burial plot until a couple of years ago with me. This was over thirty years later.

When we returned, we drove over to the cemetery and parked near a trail head. She was hoping that this was the trail she walked on all those years before. We searched on one trail, then another, and at times off it. We sauntered through the trees in the forest and found what we thought was the place, but she was not entirely convinced. Something was amiss although we took into account that the forest could have changed through the many long seasons of the decades that have passed.

We left somewhat satisfied but decided to return at a later date to be sure. We continued our exploration until we found it. It was the very place she buried her son, and she knew it!

What is remarkable is that same clearing in the trees was still evident. It was the place where the forest opened up, allowing any onlooker to direct their gaze down the hill to the children's cemetery.

After all of these years she was able to see this marvel again, and she had a witness. I saw it with her.

Seeing Timmy

I encourage my clients to engage in a daily spiritual practice, such as the many forms of meditation. From a Christian perspective, this is what is referred to as being in or practicing the presence of God.

I will even spend part of a session guiding my clients through a meditation or breathing exercise. I will have them consider what they see, a visualization that may come up while they are in a deeper brain state. I may ask, "What do you sense or see?" This is not guided imagery because we are relying on what is provided by the Divine Spirit to the client's spirit.

During one of our meetings, I had this woman go into prayerful visualization. She was able to clearly see Christ. I had her ask if Timmy was with the Lord, and she was able to confirm he was. I asked her to look around in this visualization in order to see Timmy. She saw Christ and her son holding hands, but they were facing the other direction.

She was grateful for this vision yet disheartened that she was not able to see her son's face. She took this in and was pleased with what the Divine revealed to her. She found comfort that she saw Timmy with Jesus and that her son was in safekeeping.

She repeated to me often that she wanted to see Timmy's face. And then, during one of our sessions, she reported to me that she had a dream. In this dream, she was able to see Timmy very clearly and see his face perfectly.

There was something different, however. Timmy was older, possibly seven or eight. What was presented to her was his eternal self. Or perhaps it was the precise image she needed to see. This provided her with immense solace, and she savors this visualization in her heart to this day.

It is my belief that true reality from the wider world of the beyond can be accessed through our imagination. This comes to us through our spirit—the true self—and is where the timeless domain of eternity is apprehended. This occurs most frequently through dreams and visions, often at night but also, at times, during the day.

I believe that we are guided and instructed the most when our subconscious mind is more available to us, such as in the deeper brain states of sleep or rest. Meditation or trance are fine ways to encounter other wider realities. When this occurs at night, our spirits are alive whether or not we are aware of it. I believe we are very active at night, and this may very well be when our spirits travel through the worlds.

This would behoove all of us to become more adept at seeing into the spiritual realms and to learn how to access the subconscious through dreams and visions via altered states. This stands in contrast to our typical brain state of being hyper alert and having heightened stress.

There is no greater comfort to those who have lost children on the physical plane than to know that their precious child is alive and well on the spiritual plane. To know this and believe it is one thing, yet to see it is a confirmation that provides immense joy.

The Bench

It was about this time that I was able to find a company that makes memorial benches, so I made contact. This woman and I spent some time poring over the many options on their website. We finally found the perfect bench and called the company to order it. In a matter of weeks, the bench arrived. We had some friends carry it up the hill to the very place where she buried her son on that heartbreaking night so many years ago.

She now has a memorial bench in that location to remember Timmy. And what about that gap in the trees pointing to where the other children are? It is still there. Now anyone is able to sit on that bench and look through the opening in the forest to the direction of the children's cemetery. Timmy is now with the other children who have passed.

Over time, more people have come to know about Timmy and his short life. Many have traipsed through that area of the forest to honor Timmy. We also honor his mother for what she had been through and who she has become.

During one of our sessions together, she mentioned that she did not have a birth certificate for Timmy; neither was his death registered. She was lamenting that her precious son had no identifying documentation to prove his existence. No one would know about him unless she told the story, and for so long she couldn't because of the circumstances of her life.

In that conversation, I very clearly heard these words: "Timmy is registered in heaven." I knew that the Divine Spirit sent these words. I immediately reported them to her, and she was heartened.

His time here was short-lived, and there was little or no record of his life. But Timmy is a full-fledged citizen of eternity living out his destiny there. That is why I refer to Timmy as a son registered only in heaven, and so does his mother.

6
Freedom

Austria

Following the murder of her darling baby boy, Marcos still had her in his clutches. He continued to personally use and abuse her until she graduated from high school and moved away. Nonetheless, no matter where she went, he continued to track her for the next several years.

It was about seven or eight months following Timmy's death and her graduation from high school in 1987. I asked her how she felt during this period of her life, and she wrote this:

> "Horrible. Timmy gave me a purpose, now that purpose was gone. It had been taken from me. I knew that if I had any chance of getting out for good, I needed to stick it out and graduate. So I did. I buckled down and far exceeded my own expectations and abilities and graduated."

She also expressed to me that at the time she felt like a failure. This was so often the case with abuse victims. They feel shamefully wrong, like they failed, with all the events committed by the perpetrator weighing heavily on their conscience as if they were the true violator.

After high school she was able to secure a scholarship as a Rotary Youth exchange student. She traveled to and lived in Austria for a little over a year. She attended classes in Austria and went to a language school to learn German. She was associated with an equestrian riding school and said it was truly amazing to learn what life was like in another country.

She recalls having the sense that she was totally disconnected from her life back home. It must have been very comforting to pretend that her former life did not exist.

Yet, in just a matter of time, Marcos found her. He traveled all the way to Europe to continue his harassment of her. She said, "By then I knew much more about that area and had gotten to know many of the locals that they kept me safe." Consequently, he wasn't able to abuse her as he had in the past.

Nonetheless, that Marcos was able to skip across continents to find her led her to conclude that she would never be safe as long as that murderer was alive.

Wyoming and New Mexico

After her time in Europe, she went to college in Laramie, Wyoming. She secured a ski scholarship, which helped pay for her education. She told me she skied every day of the week and loved that time immensely.

She worked several jobs while in college, including being a bartender at a cowboy bar. She also drove stock trucks into Cheyenne and was a ski instructor at a nearby ski hill. She did have what she referred to as her "night job," but she had control over this and chose her clients.

She once told me that she went back to prostitution in college because it was familiar and she could choose her clients. These encounters were less about sex and more about physical and emotional comfort.

Many of the clients didn't want sex, but they wanted to connect with and spend time with someone. She said that at times, during those long conversations, the men would fall asleep on her lap. It was like friendship, and she became friends with a lot of them. She felt like she gained as much as they did. What she was forced into as an adolescent was something she went back to in a way that benefited her and them. She made it something good through her own choice.

It was during this time when her parents divorced. Consequently, she started to drink heavily, and her alcohol use spun out of control.

Marcos, of course, found her in Wyoming as well. She once told me, "He followed me to college in Laramie and taunted me and stalked me. It was horrible." It was uncanny how he kept finding her, not only in Europe but also in Wyoming. There was no place where she could hide from him.

Marcos would make his presence known in various sadistic ways. He once siphoned the gas from the tank in her car, leaving it empty and unable to drive. There were countless times he left lifeless animals in places that would be obvious to her. He would leave dead animals on her doorstep or in her car. She found a dead cat and a dead rabbit on her doorstep on separate occasions. He once put a dead squirrel in her car. One time he snuck into her house and put a dead bird on her pillow.

On one occasion he found her at a stop light, opened her car door and punched her. He left her notes saying things like "I watched you last night." He even broke into her house once and raped her. There was frequent enough sexual contact between them during this time that she became pregnant again with another child by Marcos.

Of course, Marcos did not like it that she became pregnant. He also killed this child, but this time the child was still in her womb. He inserted a screwdriver inside of her to make sure this baby would not live.

Unraveling

It was at this time when her life began to tear apart at the seams. Her abusive drinking continued, and she was having difficulty managing her life and her emotions. She was put on academic probation and eventually lost her scholarship because she missed so much school. She eventually had to drop out of college.

In one of her drinking episodes she was so angry at everything and everyone that she bought seven bottles of tequila. She wondered how much she would have to drink to not feel anything. So she started drinking and driving. She had no destination, but she decided to drive north. She remembers going through three bottles, but her memory stopped after that.

She presumably lost her ability to drive and wrecked her car. Someone found her on the side of the road on the ground and assumed she was dead. They drove her to the hospital and found that she was still alive, so they made attempts to revive her. They attended to her for two weeks until she woke up from her alcohol-induced coma. She had no identification on her, so they treated her like a Jane Doe.

After a couple of days, she was discharged. They gave her enough money to get a bus ticket for home. She used that on Wild Turkey whiskey because she was done with tequila for obvious reasons. She then hitchhiked home.

Following this incident, she first lived with her mother. The intention was for her to provide care for her mother. This was short-lived because they could not get along. She then went to live with her father and his girlfriend, who eventually became her stepmom.

Coming back to her hometown after her travels must have been disappointing, to say the least. Yet what was paramount on her mind was getting back on her feet and putting her life back together. All the while she had one eye open for the sadistic creature who wouldn't leave her alone.

The Incident

There is something else I would like you to know about. A particular event occurred in early 1986, while this woman was still in high school. This means the incident occurred well before the post-high school events described in this chapter. It speaks of her emancipation, although temporarily, so I included it here.

She was employed as a delivery driver for a local pizza business. One night she went out on a call to deliver a pizza. Of course, she had no idea who she was delivering it to. She went to the address given and, with pizza in hand, knocked on the door. Much to her horror the person who answered the door was Marcos.

He pulled her into the apartment and locked the door behind her. He was in a rage and kept discussing past events, blaming her for everything and telling her how worthless she was. This went on for quite a while, with him berating her and speaking demeaning things to her. Even more, he hit her numerous times and physically abused her in various ways, terrifying and taunting her.

He stripped off her clothes and tied her to the bed. He told her that he was going to kill her very slowly to make sure she felt utmost pain. He then raped her. Marcos also cut her open with a knife in the genital area. He pulled out a revolver and put a couple of bullets in the chamber. He said, "We're going to play Russian roulette pussy style." He continued to rape her and beat her for what she guesses was about two hours.

Marcos put the gun inside of her vagina and pulled the trigger numerous times. Much to her surprise, the gun didn't go off. As he played his sadistic game provoking her with the gun, he raped her in between each episode. He would go back and forth from raping her to putting the gun between her legs and pulling the trigger.

During this entire time, she was kept tied up. He had several knives laid out, apparently to use at some point or to at least threaten her and keep her in a state of abject horror. It worked. She had no idea what he had planned with the knives, but she didn't want to wait long enough to find out.

Somehow, she was able to wiggle one of her hands free. She grabbed the closest knife to her and stabbed Marcos in the stomach. While he was writhing in pain, trying to determine how to care for his wound, she escaped. She grabbed her clothes and ran out the door. She put her clothes back on and went back to work. She told her boss that she was attacked and that she didn't want to go back there again.

In reflecting on the above incident at Marcos's apartment, she does not know how or why she survived. There were two bullets in a six-chamber gun. She knows because she watched him put the bullets in the gun.

Marcos clicked it five times, and each time she thought that would be it and her life would be over. He spun the chamber each time, so as to make each click of the trigger randomized. He had every intention to kill her, but the gun never went off. She is still to this day amazed that her life was spared.

The End of It All

She told me that it was quiet for a while after the above incident, but Marcos came back with a vengeance. There was more abuse that she had to endure. It seemed as if it would never end.

She wrote, "He was fixated on me," and "I couldn't get rid of him." She had been under that man's clutches for nearly eight years, and he was relentless in his pursuit of her and ruthlessly brutal in his abuse of her.

She said, "I don't know why he didn't just let me go" and "He never let it go." This was true until he did let it go. There was a point where the harassment by Marcos ended.

The abuse and taunting ended, but she still lived in fear that he would come back into her life and continue the harassment. The fear of his return lasted for decades. She was fearful everywhere she went, always suspicious and terrified for her life and safety. Yet he never returned.

You Receive What You Need Because You Ask

There is a verse in the New Testament that reads in this way:

"You do not get what you want, because you do not ask God. Or when you ask, you do not receive because you ask with the wrong motives.
You want things so you can use them for your own pleasures" (1).

The way I respond to this verse is not in the negative as it is offered but in the positive. If it is possible to not get what you want owing to certain conditions, there must be other conditions that would lead to receiving what you desire. If there is a way that is spelled out that leads to not receiving, is there another way that leads to gaining what you are longing for? If there is a way to not ask or to ask with the wrong motives, there must be a way to ask with pure intentions that leads to timely receiving.

To arrive at a place where you have a question that leads to the highest good of all, with the most honorable intentions, then asking God for what is needed will lead to gaining what you desire.

I believe that there is a vast spiritual world full of spiritual beings who are not conspiring against us but rather are conspiring for us. God, the

Spirit, the source, the creator, the higher mind; the archangels, angels, masters, teachers, and our loved ones all span the vast spiritual landscape. The Holy Bible refers to the inhabitants of this vast realm as "the cloud of witnesses" (2).

All these beings are acutely aware of us and our lives and want to help us. We have so many helpers, so many with us and around us. Knowing that there is an ample supply of helpers, we can ask any question with the best intentions and receive an answer from the divine realm.

With this in mind, during one of our sessions together this woman and I entered a calm state of mind to receive a specific answer. We had unabashed confidence that we would receive an answer.

What we wanted to know was whether or not Marcos was alive. The answer we received was no, he was no longer alive. Marcos was dead, and he could no longer bring any harm to her. She could release any lingering fear that he would find her again and bring harm to her and her family.

And that was that. The life and times of the horrible monster named Marcos was over. All the years of savage abuse and near-death assaults was finished. At long last, she was free.

The door of her cage of imprisonment was open, and she could escape to her freedom. Whether or not she chose to live a life of freedom or recreate her captivity was up to her. The next chapter will reveal her choice between living in freedom or continuing to believe that she was entrapped by her sense of unworthiness, shame, and fear.

1. James 4:2–3 (Expanded Translation)
2. Hebrews 12:1

7
Unholy Matrimony

Another Introduction to Treachery

Just three years following her high school graduation, at the age of twenty-one, she moved out and lived in a trailer park on her own. It was at this time when she decided that she needed to start going to church.

She called a particular church in a nearby town and was able to talk to the pastor about attending his church. He said there was a man who lived near her who attended this church. The pastor, who was concerned that she would have to go to the church unescorted, said that this man would pick her up and provide transportation. The man came to her trailer, picked her up, and drove her to church.

She remembers that this man was really quiet for most of the car ride to church. However, not long into the ride, he turned, looked at her, and proclaimed, "I just want you to know that I need another frustrated female in my life like I need a hole in the head."

She looked at him and retorted, "Buddy, you are just my ride to church, so drive on." After church this man took her to dinner and a month later, he proposed. In a short matter of time, she became pregnant, so they were married.

Marriage to Another Monster

I'm going to call this man Asinus. That is not his real name; it has been changed to hide his identity. Asinus, by the way, is Latin for fool.

She married Asinus in 1990 at the ripe young age of twenty-one. Somehow, mysteriously or not, she found another monster to abuse her. How that happened is hard to articulate. I have my thoughts on this, but I will leave that explanation for another time.

During their marriage, that man eventually became a pastor of a church. All the while as he performed that role, he abused his wife throughout the many years of their marriage.

For the duration of their marriage that man hit her, punched her, kicked her, threw her down on the floor or stairs, and shoved her into walls and other objects. I am not certain what he didn't do to harm her body and being. His severe abuse occurred several times a week for over twenty-five years. This is referred to as physical abuse.

He was also verbally abusive, speaking down to her with such disrespect and cruelty that she felt unloved, unworthy, and unvalued. This is known as emotional and mental abuse.

Each time they had sex over those long years, it was for him, not her. There was no nurturing or kind care in the joining of physical bodies so that love is celebrated. Rather, it was demanding, forceful, and violent. Physical, emotional, and verbal abuse occurred in the context of this sexual exploitation. This is sexual abuse, also known as rape. This is possible even in the context of marriage.

So let me repeat: Her husband was physically, emotionally, mentally, and sexually abusive to her in their marriage. All the while he was and still is a pastor of a church, leading a congregation of believers, preaching sermons, and teaching bible study. The duplicity of a so-called man of God is appalling and disturbing.

In her own words, she wrote, "Do you know how many times I prayed for the **Little House on the Prairie** life? I used to dream about living like that and having a husband that loved me and would spend time with the kids, etc."

Incidents of Abuse

Week after week, over those long years of seeing this woman in counseling, I heard unending accounts of her husband's abuse of her. She was able to separate from him on a few occasions, but she returned home to her abusive husband too many times. During one of the times that she left, he found her. She reported the following to me in her own words:

> "In December I had a run in with (Asinus). He followed me around town, and I finally ended up at the high school. There was a game going on that night so I figured that it would be a safe place for me to be. I was wrong. I got out of my car, and he came up behind me and started accosting me. He ended up throwing me down the cement embankment on the rocks. I twisted my ankle so bad I couldn't walk. He left quickly, and I went in to see (a friend at the school). He wrapped my ankle and gave me some ice. He then made sure the parking lot was safe and walked me out to my car. I called (the athletic director) to see if the surveillance cameras were working that night. They were, but they were pointing in the other direction toward the gym. I went to the police station to let them know what happened. Then I went home."

She found out through x-rays that her ankle was fractured. She wore a boot and then a brace for almost two months.

The following is a note that I wrote after one of our sessions:

> "Client said that she went to church on Sunday and her husband was really sweet and nice, and begged her to come home. She did, and in the early morning on Monday he brutally raped her and physically violated her. She said it lasted for well over an hour. He dragged her outside on the porch, stripped her naked, and then sexually aggressed himself on her. At one point when he made her suck his penis, she gagged, so he beat her on her head.

> She is a woman of her word, especially when she shakes on it with a promise. I had her pledge to never go home again when he is there and to report these incidents to law enforcement by this afternoon. We shook hands on this, and she promised. She will provide report to me through the week about her progress on these matters. She did stay away from the house the last two nights."

She reported versions of abuse like this very often. As she unraveled the extent of her entrapment in sexual slavery as a child, which you have read about in previous chapters, she also revealed the current extent of abuse in her marriage. Her therapy and my work with her required a response on two fronts: overcoming the trauma of her abusive history and managing her current traumatic experience with marital abuse.

For her to live this life and somehow endure it for not a short amount of time but over long, protracted years of incessant abuse is beyond words. How one individual could endure such treatment is more than sad, and it pierces my heart. How another person could commit such egregious crimes of horrific abuse against another, especially against one you claim to love, is beyond my ability to comprehend.

Warning Signs of Abuse

This woman once handed me a piece of paper. On this paper was a list of the warning signs of abuse. They are as follows:

> Controlling and manipulative behavior
> Verbal and mental (psychological) abuse
> Past history of abuse
> Making decisions about what you wear and where you go
> Extreme jealousy
> Always wanting to know where you are and/or who you are with
> Displaying extreme/unreasonable anger about other relationships
> Isolation from family and friends

Name-calling
Breaking or striking objects
Destroying a gift given to you by a special relative or friend
Putting their fist through a wall
Abandoning you in strange places
Pushing you out of a moving car
Threats of violence
Use of cruelty and force
Pushing, slapping, hitting, punching, kicking, or strangling

As I looked at that sheet of paper, I observed that she had circled every one of the descriptions except for one, and she had drawn a line through strangling. So her husband had never strangled her, and he had not abandoned her in strange places. Everything else on the list, he had committed against her over those long years of their marriage.

I would also like to report that This woman's husband is revered and admired in their community. He is a charismatic person who presented himself well and was liked by many. This is what halted her from letting others know about what happened behind closed doors in their home. She feared no one would believe her because his public persona provided no hint of his torture and abuse.

Why She Stayed

Here is a poem entitled "Why She Stayed" by Nikita Gill.

> He is a storm,
> And storms devastate
> But every time he hurts you
> You hold your breath
> And bear the hurricane
> Repeating to yourself,
> One more chance,
> One more breath,
> Just one more,
> And you'll fix him

> Until one day you can't
> Hold your breath anymore
> And you are
> Half a stormy evening,
> One tear-stained night,
> Two minutes
> And five seconds
> Away from breaking down.
>
> And you realize,
> You cannot fix anyone,
> Not until you fix yourself.

To this day, she is not certain why she stayed with him for all those years. She had so much fear and shame in staying, but just as much fear and shame in any prospect of leaving. Yet, in choosing to fix herself, she has begun to grow, which resulted in liberation.

Abusers and the Abused

Consider the following from the National Coalition Against Domestic Violence: (https://ncadv.org/statistics)

- Twenty people per minute are physically abused by an intimate partner in the United States.
- One in four women and one in nine men experience severe intimate partner physical violence, intimate partner contact, sexual violence, and/or intimate partner stalking.
- One in three women and one in four men have experienced some form of physical violence by an intimate partner. This includes a range of behaviors, such as slapping, shoving, and pushing and, in some cases, might not be considered domestic violence.
- One in ten women has been raped by an intimate partner. Data is unavailable on male victims.

- One in four women and one in seven men have been a victim of severe physical violence (e.g., beating, burning, strangling) by an intimate partner in his/her lifetime.
- One in seven women and one in eighteen men have been stalked by an intimate partner during her/his lifetime to a point where they felt very fearful or believed that she/he or someone close to her/him would be harmed or killed.
- Women between the ages of 18–24 are most commonly abused by an intimate partner.
- Only 34 percent of people who are injured by intimate partners receive medical care for their injuries.
- One in five women and one in seventy-one men in the United States has been raped in their lifetime.
- Almost half of female (46.7 percent) and male (44.9 percent) victims of rape in the United States were raped by an acquaintance. Of these, 45.4 percent of female rape victims and 29 percent of male rape victims were raped by an intimate partner.
- Seventy-two percent of all murder-suicides involve an intimate partner; 94 percent of the victims of these murder suicides are female.
- One in fifteen children is exposed to intimate partner violence each year, and 90 percent of these children are eyewitnesses to this violence.

You may call the National Domestic Violence Hotline for anonymous, confidential help that is available 24/7 at 1-800-799-7233 (SAFE) or 1-800-787-3224 (TTY).

The National Coalition Against Domestic Violence (NCADV) offers the following on their website:

> "Anyone can be an abuser. They come from all groups, cultures, religions, economic levels, and backgrounds. They can be your neighbor, your pastor, your friend, your child's teacher, a relative, a coworker—anyone. It is important to note that majority of abusers are only violent

with their current or past intimate partners. One study found that 90 percent of abusers do not have criminal records and abusers are generally law-abiding outside the home."

Abusers often display the following common characteristics:

- An abuser often denies the existence or minimizes the seriousness of violence and its effect on the victim and other family members.
- An abuser objectifies the victim and often sees them as their property or sexual objects.
- An abuser has low self-esteem and feels powerless and ineffective in the world. He or she may appear successful, but internally they feel inadequate.
- An abuser externalizes the cause of their behavior. They blame their violence on circumstances such as stress, their partner's behavior, a bad day, alcohol, drugs, or other factors.
- An abuser may be pleasant and charming between periods of violence and is often seen as a nice person by others outside the relationship.

The warning signs are the following:

- Extreme jealousy
- Possessiveness
- Unpredictability
- A bad temper
- Cruelty to animals
- Verbal abuse
- Extremely controlling behavior
- Antiquated beliefs about roles of women and men in relationships
- Forced sex or disregard of their partner's unwillingness to have sex
- Sabotage of birth control methods or refusal to honor agreed-on methods
- Blaming the victim for anything bad that happens

- Sabotage or obstruction of the victim's ability to work or attend school
- Need to control all the finances
- Abuse of other family members, children, or pets
- Accusations of the victim flirting with others or having an affair
- Control of what the victim wears and how they act
- Demeaning the victim either privately or publicly
- Embarrassment or humiliation of the victim in front of others
- Harassment of the victim at work

In going over the lists with her, she agreed that many, if not all, of those items were evident in her marriage. I am choosing to spare the details of what her husband had done to her and not report any more specifics in this writing.

What may be the most important thing is to raise awareness about the prevalence of abuse of all kinds. It occurs at such an alarming rate, and it must be acknowledged here so that it will stop.

It is also important for anyone reading this who is in an abusive relationship to begin to consider their own story and to get help. Please call the hotline number above or e-mail me at tomstewardpa@gmail.com or call +1-505-412-0010. Please.

A Slow and Methodical Disentanglement

During my time working with this woman in therapy, she took a cautious and careful jaunt from entire capture by her husband to sweet freedom. She had many false starts with numerous separations, only to return home to him. There were short stints away from their home, and there were longer periods away from this abusive relationship.

She finally separated permanently from her abusive husband and filed for divorce. At the time of this writing, they have mediation scheduled, and soon they will sit before a judge. Then her marriage to the latest monster in her life will be over. I am so proud of her for taking these steps.

But this has not stopped her estranged husband, Asinus, from harassing her and stalking her, even at the time of this writing. I have feared for her life and safety on countless occasions. There had been instances when he gained access to verbally and emotionally and mentally abuse her. He had also found her in certain places and had physically abused her in brutal ways. He had also cornered her because she was not careful, and he had raped her, forcing her to have sex with him.

This does not occur as frequently as when they were married, but it does happen on a regular enough basis to keep her in fear and piss me the hell off. Yeah, I get angry about it all.

Raped by the Estranged

The last time Asinus raped her was on January 30th of 2019. This was her 50th birthday.

This is the account of the story that she told me. That evening, Asinus came to her house. He knocked on the door, she opened, and he pushed his way in. Initially he was nice, and he wished her a happy birthday. He started to get more demanding, blaming her for all that was going on. Everything that happened and was occurring was her fault, particularly why they were not together. He also blamed her for him not having sex and having no one to take care of all his needs. He became physical with her, grabbing her and hitting her, and then pushed her down on the bed.

He then raped her. He forced her into sex without her consent by threatening her and physically overpowering her. He got what he wanted. She received what she didn't want, which was more trauma and shame.

She said she just wanted him to get it over with, so she didn't fight back. Regarding the duration of the rape, she said that "it was a long time." Afterward they talked for a while, but it wasn't a pleasant conversation. He was very angry, and he let her know it. He then left. She surmises that he was likely there for at least two hours, possibly more.

She was so horrified and ashamed. Her feelings of being devalued and uncared for surfaced again. The post-traumatic symptoms she had been carrying around for decades arose once more. She felt so defeated, so weak, seemingly without the strength or resolve to carry on.

However, her response to this event was smart. In the early hours of the morning, after Asinus left her, she drove to the hospital's emergency room in our town and told them what happened. They examined her violated body as they do in a rape situation and reported this event to law enforcement. She told me that they examined her "inside and out," looked at every part of her body, and asked her a lot of questions. She said the experience was very humiliating, and she felt very uncomfortable being reminded of it.

After the rape, Asinus, on the other hand, was able to go home and presumably sleep soundly in his comfortable bed with no thought that his actions were harmful and illegal.

The hospital notified local law enforcement. Since the rape occurred in an adjacent county, it was cross-reported to that county; but once again there was minimal response. She never received the result of the hospital examination even though she called several times.

In all the times that law enforcement was alerted, she was interviewed and a report was documented. Asinus was also interviewed, which resulted to nothing and served more to alert him to what she was doing to defend herself. He would then get mad and abuse her again.

Authorities provided her with options, and she had to make a choice every time what she would do. She chose not to press charges against Asinus because it would expose not only him but her as well. She was deeply fearful that her life would be dismantled in every way and that the community she had lived in her for most of her entire life would judge her for all that had occurred. She chose instead to endure the abuse, hoping it would end soon.

The Impossible Pregnancy and Unbearable Illnesses

A few weeks after the rape incident, she told me that she was pregnant. She eventually found out she was carrying triplets. She was a fifty-year-old woman with three babies in her belly, impregnated by a man who raped her on her birthday, the very disgusting man she was trying to get away from. There are a lot of ways to celebrate being alive for half a century, but this is not one of the better ones.

She never told Asinus that she was pregnant, and he does not know to this day that he impregnated her as a result of him raping her on her 50th birthday. For him, he was just getting sex from his wife, which he was entitled to. I am sure he doesn't believe he did anything wrong.

To say the least, she was devastated and bewildered to find out she was pregnant. This was another addition to the long string of traumatic crises in her life. Yet there was more to come.

Her physician ordered medical tests to check if she had heart complications. The medical tests, which included an EKG and a heart monitor, determined that she had a very healthy and functioning heart, yet it was working overtime. Her heart rate was found to be very high with a resting pulse rate between 109 to 121 beats per minute, spiking at times to the 140s.

During the medical evaluation for her heart, another abnormality was detected, and a diagnosis of sickle cell anemia was made. The following is the definition of sickle cell anemia, a genetic disorder of the blood: "Sickle cell disease is a group of disorders that affects hemoglobin, the molecule in red blood cells that delivers oxygen to cells throughout the body. People with this disorder have atypical hemoglobin molecules called hemoglobin S, which can distort red blood cells into a sickle, or crescent, shape" (1).

With the sickling of red blood cells, they break down prematurely, causing anemia. Sickle cell anemia results in a low number of red blood cells and is associated with chronic infections and multiple kinds of pain, particularly severe bone pain, which this woman has had since childhood. The sickled red blood cells become stiff and inflexible and get stuck in small blood vessels. This deprives tissues and organs of oxygen-rich blood and can lead to organ damage, particularly in the lungs, kidneys, spleen, and brain. High blood pressure in the blood vessels that supply the lungs can occur, potentially leading to pulmonary hypertension and even heart failure.

During the course of her treatment over the months following her diagnosis for sickle cell disease, she received two blood transfusions. The blood transfusions were the first order of treatment. The blood transfusions served to replace blood with sickle cells with healthy blood.

During this phase of treatment, it was also discovered that this woman had another medical complication: uterine cancer. This was another tragic blow to her life that shocked her. Treatment for her cancer included radiation, which counteracted the effect of the blood transfusions, so the transfusions needed to be halted.

Treatment for uterine cancer included a full hysterectomy, which was impossible because she was pregnant. Another option was radiation, which was also limited because of her pregnancy. She decided to take the option of a limited radiation treatment because she wanted to keep her babies.

The doctors were insistent that she terminate the pregnancy not only because of the cancer but also because of her age. They simply did not believe a fifty-year-old woman was a good candidate for triplets, especially with all of her life-threatening medical conditions.

This woman, on the other hand, had no desire to end the life of her children. She did not want to lose them and definitely didn't want to make the willful choice to end their lives. She had been there before, and it reminded her of when someone else took it upon himself to end the life of a child in her womb.

But before the radiation treatment began, she miscarried all three babies over the course of a few weeks. First, one of the babies died, which threatened the life of the other two, who eventually lost their fight for life. As you can imagine, there was so much more to this story than what could be written here, but the details will be spared.

She has strong feelings toward the doctors because she felt like they tricked her and took the life inside of her. Their intention was to save her life, but she felt significant angst and sorrow at the loss of her three babies.

And then there are her daughters. She raised three amazing young women who are accomplished and valuable contributors to the world in which they live.

The Holy Offering of Well-Preserved Daughters

This woman's daughters are young adults now, all in their twenties. They have lived a good life—safe, free, and protected during their formative years—unlike their mother. They were not subject to any harm or endangerment, she made sure of that.

These young women know nothing of her past as a sexual slave. They do not know that they have a brother who lived a year and a half and was murdered. They also do not know the extent of their father's abuse toward their mother.

How do they not know these things? Because their mother was fierce in her attempts to keep them preserved. She had been afraid for their safety ever since they were born, and she did not want harm to come to them.

She knew there was a murderer out there who presented potential danger, and she was vigilant in protecting them. She knew young girls could be sold into the sex trade, and she was not going to let that happen to her daughters. She knew her husband was an abuser of all kinds, but there was no way she would let him abuse her girls. He could abuse her, but not them.

All that her daughters knew was that for some reason their parents had separated and would likely divorce. Growing up, they knew their father was mean, moody, demanding, and unreasonable, yet he did not lay a hand on them. If he did, she would have responded with fury. She did everything she could to protect them from anyone and everyone, even when she did not extend the effort to protect herself.

I have made countless requests to this woman to tell her daughters about what had occurred. So far she has told them nothing. I respect this wish. I know offering the grisly truth would be very difficult for her. Consequently, she has chosen to not tell anyone in her family about these matters. This is also why her identity is concealed. This writing is a memoir of the nameless, yet I am certain that this offering can still have a powerful impact.

A Summary of the Unbearable

So, just to pull it all together, this woman was in tremendous physical and emotional pain because of incidents of abuse and illness throughout her entire life. She had been abused physically, emotionally, mentally, and in every which way imaginable. She had been sexually used, violated, and assaulted since she was a child. Her body carried considerable pain, which was often too much to bear. To top it off she was diagnosed with sickle cell anemia and uterine cancer.

And oh yeah, she became pregnant after being raped by her abusive husband. A fifty-year-old woman carrying triplets! Then she lost her babies and was forced to mourn yet another loss. All in all, she miscarried five babies, two in her marriage and the three just mentioned. She had two of her children taken from her through murder, one inside the womb and one outside. That's ten babies in total from eight pregnancies.

How did she do it? How was she able to walk that tragic path of pain and suffering? Her recovery and healing is what will be revealed in the coming chapters.

1. https://ghr.nlm.nih.gov/condition/sickle-cell-disease#synonyms

8
Ambrosia's Subtle Soothing

Drinking to Survive

What has been mentioned in this woman's story is a reliance on alcohol since her adolescent years. Who could blame her?

She once wrote to me: "I do truly enjoy my whiskey. I can justify it very well, but when it comes right down to it, justified or not, I have to ask myself, 'Is this truly what will help me in the long run?' My ideal situation is get up, have a couple shots before breakfast, chase it with several cups of coffee, have a nice breakfast, then go to work. Maybe a few more at lunch, then a few more right before bedtime, then I sleep like a baby! And it's worked like that for quite some time until a major event happens, then I go on a binge and can down a bottle in a day."

She learned to drink as a teenager to deal with the horrendous abuse she was forced to endure as a victim of sexual trafficking. When she delivered Timmy all by herself in the bathtub, whiskey was at her side. When she buried Timmy, whiskey was her trusted companion. When her parents divorced, her emotions flooded forth and all she knew to do was turn to alcohol. So many instances in her life initiated her reliance on the subtle soothing of that scintillating liquid.

Along the way she developed an all-too-strong reliance on that magic elixir. Whiskey was her ambrosia, the sustenance of the gods. It was the solution, a pain reliever for her aching bones and an aphrodisiac for her tattered heart, with its soundless nuances and reverberations.

As she became reluctantly honest with me about her drinking, I grew very concerned about the extent of her overuse. What I was able to determine was that her weekdays routinely went like this: She would buy a fifth of whiskey at about seven o'clock in the morning at the local supermarket. She would mix her whiskey with 7 Up in her big cup and sip on it for most of the day.

She did this for over twenty years. She didn't drink as much on the weekends because her husband and children would find out. So she was mostly a weekday drinker, picking herself up throughout the day. In her estimation, she would not have been able to make it through otherwise.

The Phone Call

My concern grew to an extent that during one of her sessions with me I had her call a treatment center nearby. I didn't want to tell her to make that call on her own time because she most likely wouldn't have done it. I also wanted her to make the call to show her initiative. I gave her the number while in my office and asked her to get her phone out and call. In her typical dutiful fashion, she complied.

As usual, she was not as detailed about the extent of her drinking as I would have liked. She did tell the intake counselor enough about her practices that she was told to get herself into an inpatient program as soon as possible. Her drinking was determined to be serious enough to warrant immediate inpatient treatment. She needed exhaustive detoxification and close monitoring through the entire process of coming off alcohol.

She was also told that there was no way that she could quit drinking on her own. The extent of her drinking was severely impacting her health that even stopping the consumption of alcohol would present serious health risks. She needed help and she needed it soon. The only option she had was to admit herself voluntarily and immediately. This was the result of a phone assessment by a professional chemical dependent counselor.

When she got off the phone, we looked at each other. I knew the counselor was right, and so did she. I also knew she wasn't going to follow through with the course of action that she was strongly urged to take. There was also no way I could make her. I sent her away that day hoping that she might, against all odds, consent to this treatment plan.

Searching for An Answer

I also wondered if there was some other plan that could be initiated that would fit with the demands of her life and her resistance, which was saturated with shame and fear. Everything had been so hard for her, so I was hoping there would be some option that was seamless yet comprehensive.

Keep in mind that she was so secretive and stealthy in her drinking; no one knew she had a serious problem. No one, not even her husband, knew the extent of her alcohol addiction. Her children never figured it out, and even though she drank at work, apparently no one she ever worked with knew.

She sipped on a whiskey cooler all day long. She never became embarrassingly drunk. Her drinking gave her a steady buzz throughout each day. This was how she dealt with it all. She only became crazy drunk every once in a while.

In most of our sessions in the first couple of years or so, I monitored her intake by asking her questions about it. She was fairly honest with me, but only if I pressed. If I didn't ask, she wouldn't tell me. Early on her drinking was, of course, very frequent. She did have some success by not drinking for periods at a time.

Being an intuitive person, there were times when I sensed the need to ask if she had anything to drink the previous week. She would look at me then and ask something like, "How did you know to ask?" I knew but had no intention of shaming her. I only wanted to bring to light what she was doing, so she knew she had a compassionate witness she could be accountable to.

She would have her binge periods so often that I remained very concerned about her drinking, in spite of the fact that she could go through periods of not drinking. I frequently considered what serious toll her drinking was having on her physiology.

I have known people in their forties, thirties, or even in their twenties who have died as a direct result of overdrinking. I often wondered if alcohol was a silent killer for this woman. She made it this far, yet I was not certain how much more time she actually had. If she didn't stop drinking, she would certainly die.

Turning Off the Mechanism to Use Alcohol

When she first came in to see me as a counselor, I had just lost a son to drug overdose. The passing of my son occurred about a year before I met this woman. This loss led me to ponder a lot about addiction.

In those early days as we were contending with her addiction to alcohol, I was still ruminating on the addictive process. What are we doing when we use or abuse substances? Why use something that can be so potentially destructive to every aspect of life and living? Why imbibe on alcohol or drugs in a way that was so detrimental to the body and could lead to premature death?

As I reflected on this, I began to consider that there must be some mechanism in the body that, when turned on, propels us to partake. I began to contemplate not only on how this mechanism could be turned on (leading to addictions) but also on how it could be switched off.

My main drive there was to somehow reconcile with the death of my son. If I have found the turn off switch to that mechanism for him, I could have saved him. Since this was not possible, perhaps I could provide a catalyst to help others.

I know it sounds like wishful and magical thinking. I know the energy behind it is the painful grief and sorrow of having a deceased son. I also know it sounds codependent or even something that borders on a messiah complex. Yet some of the greatest discoveries in the history of humankind were propelled by a similar energy, so I wasn't going to stop thinking this way no matter how silly or unhealthy it sounded.

I do realize my son was supposed to go when he did, and he would have transferred to the next life in another way if it wasn't drug overdose. Nonetheless, I continued to consider how some version of faith and a powerful intervention could alter a particular mechanism in the body via strong intention.

I have always liked prayers. I have written out my prayers like statements of intention in journals throughout the years in a way that has helped guide me in my life. I have written out these statements and prayers as healing protocols that have been used in my counseling office. I decided to write out a prayer that would initiate turning off the mechanism to abuse substances. Sounds presumptuous doesn't it? I didn't care, I was shooting for the moon. I do that.

So, I wrote out a prayer. I called it the mechanism turn off prayer. Over the years I have prayed this prayer only a few times with certain people. I was selective because I didn't want it to lose power by overdoing it (yeah, I know that's also silly). This woman was one of the people I prayed it with.

The Prayer

I want you to know that I have a history of being in Christianity and have studied many Christian healing programs. I have also been in the field of psychology for over thirty years. At the time of this writing, I have ventured into energy healing and energy psychology.

It is my longing to heal myself and others with any means available that is efficient and thorough. I don't want to waste any time if I don't have to. It is my aim to get to the source instead of floundering on surface distractions.

This reminds me of a verse from the writings of the apostle Paul. He said, "You only look at the surface of things" (1). I don't want to remain fixed on surface realities. I am driven to look deeper, to the root, source, and cause.

I have, over the years, looked at the stories in the gospels where Christ offered spectacular demonstrations of miraculous healings. These healing accounts of Christ display, from my perspective, three important qualities:

1. Voice – Christ sent out such an intense thrust of healing power through his speaking voice that significant changes occurred, which were consistent with his intention. Incredible exploits occurred in response to the powerful vibration of his utterances.

2. Energy Transfer – Healing power left Christ's body so that simply touching him or being touched by him facilitated a transfer of energy. This exchange enabled him to sense the energy leaving him and for others to sense the energy entering into them.
3. Distance Healing – Christ healed at a distance; he sent out the healing energy from his voice and intention and it traveled to distances that at times were many miles away. There was no limit as to how far this healing power could go to perform the spectacular.

In our current time, the first quality is exemplified by the growing field of energy healing where the vibration of conscious intention is expressed via the spoken word or even through thought alone. What we say, either positive or negative, is so very powerful. When we are intentional about what we express with our voice or our intentions, healing and transformation can occur.

The second characteristic is evidenced in the many healing traditions throughout the ages that recognize bioenergetics or the energy body, which includes the "biofield" (also known as the aura). There are many who sense and/or see energy in the space around them and on the bodies of others. This enables them to make an energy field assessment by connecting with the subtle body of others. Seasoned healers know when there is energy transfer, where energy leaves them in a way that is beneficial to others.

The third quality is represented by the principle of quantum entanglement in the field of physics. Two entangled objects, when separated, behave in similar ways and influence each other even when they are at considerable distances apart. As an example, I offer healing sessions to my friends and associates in the African country of Uganda. There are no limits of distance to healing potential.

I believe this is what Christ meant when he said that we not only will be able to perform the same healing exploits he presented, but we would be able to perform even greater healings than he did. We have come into a time when our ability to heal has surpassed that of Christ's, just like he said it would (2).

With this in mind, here is the healing mechanism turn off prayer:

> *By the power of Spirit and in the name of the Christ, I ask that the mechanism in _____ that switches on for _____ be turned off, and that the origin and source behind the activation of this mechanism be deleted and re-attuned. I also direct _____'s body to heal and recalibrate in reference to the harmful effects of the use of this substance. Amen; so be it.*

I have since added to this prayer to include everyone, whether he/she has a faith tradition or spiritual practice, or none at all. Here is the updated version:

> Move into a calm or altered state by meditating for a few moments or minutes.
>
> Seek guidance from the divine power source of your choosing to direct your prayer to:
>
> God, Divine, Creator, Christ, Spirit, Source, Universal Consciousness, Higher Mind, All That Is, Spiritual Guides, Self, or nothing at all, etc.
>
> Ask the spirit if there is anything you need to know, sense, see, or experience regarding the issue you are addressing in order to determine the energy behind this issue, and record any information or insights in the space below or on another document.
>
> _____
> _____
> _____
> _____
> _____
>
> And finally, are you ready, willing, and able for this particular issue to be eliminated from your life in all of its facets and forms, and for any underlying issue(s) to be exposed so that there will be no hindrance in removing its energetic charge?

After completing the above steps and while remaining in a state of meditative calm and connected to the source who will help and guide you, say this prayer:

Regarding the energetic impulse in _____ (name of person) *that switches on for* _____ (alcohol, drugs, anxiety, anger, illness, disease, addictions, compulsions, habits, etc.), *whether this energy is represented chemically, emotionally, physically, mentally, behaviorally, spiritually, or by any other means;*

And in every way that this energy presents itself and wherever this energy is stored in the body, and by whatever issue this energy presents itself and whatever source and whichever point of origin the energy may have had its beginnings,

I ask, request, and establish, by the power in and around me from _____ (choose from the above names), *that the mechanism or trigger for the above-named impulse be switched off at its source and place of origin, never to be turned on again,*

And that any harmful effects from use and engagement with this chemical or action be completely repaired so that _____*'s body, soul, and spirit, will now be healed, whole, and well.*

So be it.

The Loss of the Impulse to Drink

After we prayed the first prayer above, this woman lost her urge to drink. Poor thing. Haha!

As the mechanism was turned off, her dependence on alcohol became extremely limited. There were times when she reported that she drank yet there was no effect. She couldn't get drunk! There were times when drinking even made her feel nauseated or sick.

With this new experience with alcohol, she stopped drinking, and there were no detrimental effects from getting off alcohol in spite of her many long years of dependence. Now isn't that something?

Over time, she did return to drinking more casually, yet it was more for enjoyment than it was to obsessively chase the pain away. Okay, I'm sure she has had her moments of dependency and she has used alcohol because of pain, but it certainly wasn't like what it was before.

I'm pleased this prayer worked for her, yet I do wish it would have worked for my son. I would like to believe that my son was the driving force in providing me with the insight and impulse for this prayer.

I know he was. That's precisely how the spiritual world helps us.

1. 2 Corinthians 10:7
2. John 14:12

9
Sexual Trafficking of Children in America

The Criminal Sexual Enterprise

By now I am sure you are aware that we have a significant crisis of criminal sexuality in America. We have recently watched the emergence of the Me Too movement where many women, and also men, have come out as victims of sexual assault and sexual harassment. This has exposed the issue of sexual violation against victims as never before.

There is now an awareness of sexual excesses by individuals that may be considered more consensual. The Ashley Madison database was hacked into just a few years ago, and thirty-two million people who used the website to cheat on their spouses were put to the spotlight.

Then there is convicted sex offender Jeffrey Epstein, who "developed an elite social circle and procured women and many underage girls who were then sexually abused by Epstein and . . . his influential contacts" (1). The mystery around this man—whether he killed himself in jail or was murdered—will most likely never be solved. I believe he was murdered by the elite who had a lot to hide.

We at least know this: humans get off on sex. All sorts of sexuality occur in the adult world. There is also an extensive sexual trafficking ring involving children that is presumably associated with the upper echelons of society. This includes politicians, the clergy and so many of the self-professed untarnished. If Epstein was murdered, it was because he knew the specific names of the influential and powerful who engaged in prostitution with women of age as well as illegal sexual acts against minor girls and boys.

Helpful Organizations

We definitely have a problem in America. Children are seen as sexual objects and are too often exploited for the sexual gratification of men (and sometimes women) who believe they are simply indulging in private gratification. We need to do something other than tolerate or ignore this sexual exploitation. These acts can no longer be seen as a normal way to experience pleasure because too many children are being violated.

The following organizations and their corresponding websites are excellent resources. You may click on these links in order to delve deeper and see what is being done to end child prostitution and sexual trafficking.

>Ending the Game – https://endingthegame.com/
>Shared Hope – https://sharedhope.org
>Deliver Fund – https://www.deliverfund.org
>Prostitution research – http://prostitutionresearch.com/
>Polaris Project – https://polarisproject.org/human-trafficking/sex-trafficking
>Nordic Model Now – https://nordicmodelnow.org/
>National Human Trafficking Hotline – https://humantraffickinghotline.org/

There is also a toll-free hotline anyone may call. It is:

1 (888) 373-7888 or SMS: 233733 (Text "HELP" or "INFO")
Hours: 24 hours, 7 days a week
Languages: English, Spanish, and two hundred more

Child Sex Trafficking in the United States

The following is a summary of what can be found on the Shared Hope website:

What is known as domestic minor sex trafficking (DMST) has been defined as "the commercial sexual exploitation of children through buying, selling, or trading their sexual services . . ." which occurs through "prostitution, pornography, stripping, and other sexual acts." These acts are induced by force, fraud, coercion, or by trading sexual services for some form of compensation in order to survive, particularly while the child is living on the streets. This compensation often includes shelter, food, drugs, etc. These children are victims of sexual exploitation because they are minors even if they "chose" this lifestyle.

The traffickers or pimps recruit girls from middle school and high school campuses. Traffickers may also use social media sites to recruit potential victims. The child may be recruited from malls, parks, bus stops, shelters, and group homes. Children who are runaways are particularly susceptible to coercion. Preteens are frequent targets because they are potentially more apt to be manipulated by charm and seduction. Shared Hope has mentioned on their website that "no youth is exempt from falling prey to these tactics."

Once the child has been lured in through some form of manipulation, they will be introduced into the trade by working the streets or going into child pornography. These traffickers then use physical, emotional, and psychological abuse to force these children into the trade and also to keep them in the business. At times there is the threat of violence against them or their loved ones in order to make certain that they remained under the control of their pimp.

Those who buy sex from a minor could be anyone. There is no profile or type of individual who is exempt from engaging in child exploitation, and they come from a broad spectrum of our society. Buyers are hard to identify because their initial contact can be as little as a few minutes and they pay in cash. The primary identifying characteristic of these criminal exploiters is that they are adult males.

Child exploitation is not limited to the streets and to physical contact. Trafficking also includes pornography that can be purchased and viewed online. This version of the crime is very sadistic as children are demanded to engage in often brutal and terrorizing acts of sexual coercion.

If someone you know is being groomed for trafficking or is in the process of being trafficked, please visit sharedhope.org/report/ in order to make a report.

Recognizing the Signs

> This entire section is taken directly from https://humantraffickinghotline.org.

Are you or someone you know being trafficked? Is human trafficking happening in your community? Recognizing potential red flags and knowing the indicators of human trafficking is a key step in identifying more victims and giving them the assistance they need.

Bear in mind that not all indicators will be present in all situations. The type of trafficking, content, and environment are all important to take into account.

Common work and living conditions:
The individual(s) in question

- is not free to leave or come and go at will;
- is under eighteen and is providing commercial sex acts;
- is in the commercial sex industry and has a pimp/manager;
- is unpaid, paid very little, or paid only through tips;
- works excessively long and/or unusual hours;
- is not allowed breaks or suffers under unusual restrictions at work;
- owes a large debt and is unable to pay it off;
- was recruited through false promises concerning the nature and conditions of his/her work;
- stays in work and/or living locations with high security measures (e.g., opaque windows, boarded-up windows, bars on windows, barbed wire, security cameras, etc.);
- is living and working on-site;
- experiences verbal or physical abuse by their supervisor;
- is not given proper safety equipment;

- is not paid directly;
- is forced to meet daily quotas.

Poor mental health or abnormal behavior
The individual(s) in question

- is fearful, anxious, depressed, submissive, tense, or nervous/paranoid;
- exhibits unusually fearful or anxious behavior after bringing up law enforcement or immigration officials;
- shows signs of substance use or addiction.

Poor physical health
The individual(s) in question

- shows signs of poor hygiene, malnourishment, and/or fatigue;
- shows signs of physical and/or sexual abuse, physical restraint, confinement, or torture.

Lack of control
The individual(s) in question

- has few or no personal possessions;
- is frequently monitored;
- is not in control of their own money, financial records, or bank account;
- is not in control of their own identification documents (ID or passport);
- is not allowed or able to speak for themselves (a third party may insist on being present and/or translating).

Others
The individual(s) in question

- has claims of just visiting and inability to clarify where they are staying (address);

- shows lack of knowledge of whereabouts and/or do not know what city he/she is in;
- appears to have lost sense of time;
- shares scripted, confusing, or inconsistent stories;
- protects the person who may be hurting them or minimizes abuse.

This list is not exhaustive and represents only a selection of possible indicators. The red flags in this list may not be present in all trafficking cases. Each individual indicator should be taken in context, not be considered in isolation, nor should be taken as proof that human trafficking is occurring. Additionally, cultural differences should also be considered.

Governmental Help

Here is an excellent article on child sex trafficking from the Department of Justice that I would highly encourage you to read: https://www.justice.gov/criminal-ceos/child-sex-trafficking.

In this article, the following is offered: "The United States not only faces a problem of foreign victims trafficked into the country, but there is also a homegrown problem of American children being recruited and exploited for commercial sex."

The article begins with this statement: "Child sex trafficking refers to the recruitment, harboring, transportation, provision, obtaining, patronizing, or soliciting of a minor for the purpose of a commercial sex act. Offenders of this crime who are commonly referred to as traffickers or pimps, target vulnerable children and gain control over them using a variety of manipulative methods. Victims frequently fall prey to traffickers who lure them in with an offer of food, clothes, attention, friendship, love, and a seemingly safe place to sleep. After cultivating a relationship with the child and engendering a false sense of trust, the trafficker will begin engaging the child in prostitution and use physical, emotional, and psychological abuse to keep the child trapped in a life of prostitution. It is common for traffickers to isolate victims by moving them far away from friends and family, altering their physical appearances, or continuously moving them to new locations. Victims are heavily conditioned to remain loyal to the trafficker and to distrust law enforcement. No child is immune to becoming a victim of child sex trafficking, regardless of the child's race, age, socioeconomic status, or location, and every child involved in this form of commercial sexual exploitation is a victim."

Deputy Attorney General James Cole, at the National Strategy Conference on Combating Child Exploitation in San Jose, California, on May 17, 2011, spoke of this in his address: "Some of our most vulnerable children also face the threat of being victimized by commercial sexual exploitation. Runaways, throwaways, sexual assault victims, and neglected children can be recruited into a violent life of forced prostitution."

So there is acknowledgment and awareness in our government, and it is apprised of the presence and extent of the sexual trafficking of children in the Unites States. Yet you may be wondering what you can do.

What You Can Do

What can you do regarding the issue of the sexual exploitation of children? Peruse the above websites and become acquainted with these organizations. Subscribe to their e-mail list and support them in any way you are able. In addition, look at the people and occurrences around you in a different light, knowing that one of the children you know could be a victim or a potential victim.

You may also share this book to those who may have even a slight interest. Take this book and this topic to your churches, community groups, and social gatherings. This woman and I are willing to speak at a gathering that you may host. We hope to take this message to as many places as possible, so contact us if you have any interest.

I would encourage you to bring up this subject in the many places you find yourself. This could be at work, at home, or with friends. It would help a lot if we didn't ignore it and pretend it doesn't exist. The more we remind ourselves and others that this is a huge problem needing our attention, the faster we may begin to save our children.

There are many community groups in the US that are playing a wonderful role in providing a community and meaning to many. One of the largest institutions that has been so very helpful over time are churches, synagogues, parishes, and wards. I am grateful for their role in the education and training of our youth and adults to be better citizens.

What is most disturbing to me is the association of religious organizations with the sexual trafficking of children in the United States. In my town, two men have been arrested, jailed, and imprisoned in recent years for online pornographic sexual exploitation of children. In both cases, these men were pastors. It rocked our community to know that these men who lived among us and led our community in spiritual matters were also engaged in the criminal sexual violation of children.

This is why I believe our religious gatherings ought to expose this issue head on. It needs to be talked about in every possible context in our houses of faith. Sermons, Sunday school lessons, bible studies, discussion groups, prayer groups, etc. could present the topic of sexual exploitation of children. The purpose would be to give a wake-up call to predators or possible predators because they very likely are among us. This could also educate children to know they could easily become prey.

Please join us in these in these efforts. Again, call +1-505-412-0010 or e-mail tomstewardpa@gmail.com.

Ritual Abuse

There is something else that the woman in this story conveyed to me very recently. This is the involvement of what has come to be known as ritualistic abuse. The original term used for this was satanic ritual abuse, yet this has been altered to avoid overly religious connotations. It is referred to now as sadistic ritual abuse, or its shortened version of ritual abuse (RA). This may seem like an odd turn in a chapter about the sexual trafficking of children, yet I would like to simply state that there appears to be a correlation between these two areas.

I don't want to go into much detail about the subject of Ritual Abuse other than tell you this woman's story. Suffice it to say that RA consists of particular ceremonies that include worship of certain spirit entities and the sacrifice of very young children.

This woman told me that as a teenager, she participated with Jimmy and Marcos in strange rituals. I want to say up front that these events were not her idea, and it did not originate with her. She was coerced into these ceremonies like so many of the other acts she was forced into.

She said that most of these rituals occurred at the cemetery, at times at the ski hill or at other random locations in the mountains near our town. Monthly rituals were held, and there were important dates, like Halloween, that held special significance. There were usually about a dozen people, but on the special ceremonies there were quite a bit more. She said she didn't recognize those in attendance because those events were held "always at night so you couldn't see anyone."

These were closed-door ceremonies, and only certain people were invited. She went to three or four a year, saying that "they told me which ones to show up to." For some reason, she was not allowed at all of the rituals. This may be because of something that they didn't want her to know about.

Jimmy led these gatherings, and it was up to him what happened. She stated, "It's like they went into a trance, and they became totally different. It seemed like they were possessed or controlled by a spirit." She told me that "it smelled like death."

There was always a lot of alcohol and drugs. Additionally, there was always sex involved. Everyone engaged in sexual contact, often with multiple partners. There was sexual activity occurring all over the place, which she described as bizarre and aggressive. Her role was to be with Jimmy although he had other partners.

She said she never saw them sacrifice children although she overheard them talking about it. She was able to figure out that they sacrificed a newborn or an infant. Her friend Allison didn't want to talk about the sacrifices, and it was presumed something happened to her or one of her children.

There was one incident that she labored through deep pain to tell me about. On this particular night both Jimmy and Marcos sexually violated her over and over again, although Marcos wasn't allowed to ejaculate in her. At one point, Marcos held her back while Jimmy shoved a bottle in her vagina. They said they were trying to teach her how to be with clients. This was, of course, extremely painful, and she was in abject terror.

At one point she bit Marcos and he released her. She was then hit with the bottle and the glass shattered all over the ground. While she lay on the ground with glass puncturing her bare skin, they engaged in repeated sex acts with her. Through the pain of recalling this event she said that once they were done, they just left her there. She was able to clean herself up and get away. She said, "I had cuts everywhere, front and back and top and bottom."

What Are We Doing to Our Children?

I'm not sure what page this is in this book you are reading, but I'm proud of you for making it this far. This chapter along with some others contain graphic and difficult content. My aim here in this chapter and throughout this book is to bring to light horrible atrocities that are occurring to our children. These are not children in a faraway place that can remain nameless and faceless. These are children in our nation, our state, our town, our neighborhoods, and in some cases our families.

What are we doing to our children? More importantly, what are we going to do to help our children? How will we protect them and how will we respond? There are some suggestions in this chapter so I hope that you will follow through in some way. If you do, I would be very grateful. Thank you for reading this far.

Now, let's consider how the woman in our story experienced healing and recovery.

1. Wikipedia
2. Shared Hope International
3. Human Trafficking Online

10

Healing the Brokenhearted

At this point in the story, you know what this woman had been through. There is so much more, yet it is difficult to include everything. I believe what has been written here will help you understand enough of her story, and we can now consider her healing.

You do know this woman has experienced considerable healing, recovering from much of the emotional, psychological, and physical trauma that she has experienced. You may be wondering how this healing occurred.

Much of the healing came from her slowly and methodically telling her story to a witness. That would be me. Before me, hardly anyone knew the extent of the secrets about her former life that she held within her.

In her words: "There have only been five others who knew I had a son, most of whom helped me take care of him during the day while I was at school or work. Three knew he had died, but you are the first and only one I have ever shared the details with about his death. I have kept it so close to my heart that I didn't dare let it out. Thank you for providing a safe and trusting place for me to share."

Imagine holding this devastating secret inside your shattered heart for decades, not able or willing to tell anyone, and consequently not receiving the compassionate response that was needed the most.

In reference to what she wanted to work on in therapy, she told me many times that she wanted address her nightmares and memories, "all of the abuse growing up within the family and outside of it . . . health issues . . . all the deaths in my family . . . my drinking . . . why kids have to die . . . trust—or lack thereof—with everyone."

She has learned to trust herself and others, which has done a lot to dissipate her fear and shame. I am not the only person she revealed her story to. She eventually trusted others.

Widening the Circle

At one point I realized that an old classmate of hers from high school was still in town. This man was a friend of mine. I asked her if she remembered him. She did. I knew this man was a kind soul who could be a great source of support for her. I was simply attempting to widen her circle, so I picked someone who knew her in the earlier seasons of her life. I then made plans to connect them.

I texted her and told her that there was someone at the high school (where he worked) who would like to meet her. I didn't tell him who it was or what was her story, I just knew he was the right person.

I knew this connection would be helpful because this man and his wife lost their oldest son to a climbing accident. This loss occurred just a few months prior to this arranged meeting. That they both have lost a son would hopefully start a meaningful alliance based on shared experience.

She trusted me and went over to the high school and met this man, someone she had not seen or talked to in over thirty years. She was surprised, yet it didn't take long to establish a strong bond. They were able to reminisce about the past and also what has transpired over the decades since high school.

Over the days, weeks, months, and now years, this man proved to be compassionate enough to enable her to trust him with her story. He had been an immense support to her during this time (he was the one who arranged for Timmy's memorial bench to be placed on the hillside). He is shocked and horrified about what had happened to her and had no idea what was occurring while they were still in high school. Apparently, no one else did either.

A little over a year ago my friend Lynn and I led a grief group for those who have experienced the loss of a child. The man, his wife, and the woman in this story, along with about ten others, were the attendees of this group. It was heart-wrenching to hear their grief-laden stories, yet the support and connection that occurred for all of us was heartwarming. Some of the people in that group helped this woman widen her circle because she trusted them with at least parts of her story.

She began to tell even more people about her life. She also had more interaction with law enforcement. They have heard a lot, mostly about her current abusive marriage. What frustrates me is that little can be done regarding the abuse she received from her husband. Of course, the abuse has lessened, yet in certain ways it is still ongoing.

The story of her involvement in prostitution as a child is something that was revealed to only a certain select few. This has included the man mentioned above and his wife. I hope you realize how healing it had been for her to talk about her life experiences. As she came out of hiding and received loving care, her broken heart was sewn back together piece by piece.

Energy Healing

Many of my discussions while counseling with this woman would be considered traditional psychotherapy, which is known as talk therapy. It may also be referred to as insight-oriented therapy because it was my aim to enable her to see herself, her life, her experiences, as well as her future, in an entirely different light. This did occur.

My aim in her counseling was to facilitate not only her healing but also her freedom. As was mentioned in a previous chapter, she was like a bird in a cage. The door of her cage was recently swung open, but for a long time she did not exit and retreat to safety. Yet over time, she began to walk through the door. She now feels freer than she ever has.

She is outside the cage, yet, sad to say, her husband continues to find her and stalk her. I hope this ends soon. She is afraid it will only end on the occasion of his death or hers.

While I was counseling her, I was also developing my skills in the area of energy psychology. I learned a lot from other practitioners as I read, studied, and attended trainings, either online or in person. I then developed my own energy psychology healing protocol. It is called the Spirit Code, and you can read about it on my website (www.tomsteward.com).

During our Spirit Code sessions early on, it was determined that she had what is known as a "heart wall." This is the strategic manner in which we cover the ever-powerful yet vulnerable heart center. We all do this because we've all had traumatic experiences to some measure and we fear that further harm may come to us. Since life and the people in it were experienced as unsafe, we do all we can to protect ourselves.

This woman had experienced significant trauma, and we were able to determine that her heart wall was of a considerable size. Well, of course it was. We discovered some particular repressed emotions that comprised the covering of her heart center. These emotions had been collected over a long life of anguishing experiences, which you have read about. As these emotions were released from her body, her heart wall diminished in size significantly.

Spirit Code accounts for what we refer to as core states. The four core states in Spirit Code are fear, rage, pain, and shame. There were two core states that came up in several contexts throughout her life and were revealed in our sessions. They are, not surprisingly, shame and fear. Being able to locate these and other states of being—with the help of the Spirit—and then activating their transformation was what played a significant role in her healing.

There are other core states, which are deeper than the others mentioned. They are more positive and regenerative and can be described by the following designations: love, joy, peace, dignity, and many others. She had replaced the first list with the second, all by the work of the Spirit. These inner qualities are known in the New Testament as fruits from the Spirit (1).

The Shield

As the protective covering, or the heart wall, is removed from a person, they may feel vulnerable and exposed. We then apply what is known as a shield. The psalmist, King David, wrote the following, which is recorded in the Hebrew Bible:

> "But You, O Lord, are a shield about me,
> my glory, who holds my head high" (2).

So there is a "shield" made of the substance of the Divine that is able to cover us all over. This includes covering the heart, the most vulnerable yet powerful area in the human body There is no better means of protection when the world around us seems unsafe.

If you have manufactured any sort of fear-based flimsy covering, it needs to be removed. This covering is made up of life issues and the accompanying repressed emotional states. As you resolve old patterns, this fear-generated means of protection will begin to diminish. Then a shield made of stuff from God is installed to protect you from any and all undue harm.

This is what happened to this woman. In the presence of fear and in great danger, she sheltered herself with a protective covering that she thought would help. In some ways, it did, yet mostly it created additional problems. It took some time and many counseling sessions, but this inadequate means of protection was eventually removed from her.

We then applied a shield made from the substance of the Divine and draped it over her entire being. This enabled her heart to feel much stronger and more protected. It aided her to move from fear to love and shame to dignity in ways that permitted her to hold her head high, just like how the psalmist suggested.

Forgiveness

During our sessions together, we were guided often to consider forgiveness. She wrote this: "I do have a lot of unforgiveness inside of me" and "I know I need to deal with . . . unforgiveness."

There is such a great power in forgiveness, and for this woman it cleared out a lot of old emotional debris from within. She was able to intentionally forgive quite a few people, including all those individuals who have violated, abused, and harmed her in so many ways.

The forgiveness prayer that we use in my office goes something like this:

> "It is my intention to completely, thoroughly, and permanently forgive _____ for _____. I also choose to no longer hold anything against _____

for his/her actions or inactions. I choose instead to bless _____, and to extend love and mercy toward _____. I also ask God to bless _____, and to offer love and mercy to _____."

She had worked on forgiving her parents, Jimmy, Marcos, and others. She also needed to forgive God because for a while she had a lot of anger toward God for her life of pain. And also, very importantly, she needed to forgive herself. This was a big one. What she is considering currently is forgiveness for her husband. This is hard because in many ways it is ongoing and more current.

With forgiveness, none of that matters. You forgive the other person for you, whether or not they play a role in the process, and independent of the other person's participation or behavior. Forgiveness is so powerful, as this woman found out.

Fear is a Liar

I once asked this woman what her favorite songs and hymns were. She replied, "I have four favorite songs: one, 'The Old Rugged Cross'; two, 'El Shaddai'; three, 'Fear, He Is A Liar'; and four, 'Big, Big House'."

She was particularly moved by the song "Fear, He Is A Liar" by songwriters Jason Ingram, Zach Williams, and Jonathan Lindley Smith.

You can search for this song on YouTube and listen to it. Some of the words are included below:

> "When he told you you're not good enough,
> When he told you you're not right,
> When he told you you're not strong enough
> To put up a good fight
> When he told you you're not worthy,
> When he told you you're not loved,
> When he told you you're not beautiful,
> That you'll never be enough
> Fear, he is a liar.
> He will take your breath,

> Stop you in your steps
> Fear, he is a liar.
> He will rob your rest,
> Steal your happiness,
> Cast your fear in the fire
> 'Cause fear, he is a liar.
> When he told you were troubled,
> You'll forever be alone;
> When he told you should run away,
> You'll never find a home;
> When he told you were dirty,
> And you should be ashamed,
> When he told you could be the one
> That grace could never change
> Fear, he is a liar."

Included in this song is the following plea as a prayer to God:

> "Let your fire fall and cast out all my fears; let your fire fall, your love is all I feel. Oh, let your fire fall and cast out all my fears; let your fire fall, your love is all I feel" (3).

She had fears—so many—and she had believed lies. All of the things mentioned in that song, the lies she came to believe, had resonated within her deeply. A lot of it had been resolved in our sessions when we discussed these matters using various forms of counseling interventions.

Her conscious and subconscious belief system has been reconfigured so that fear's deception no longer resonated and pulsated within her. The song reflected this inner work by the Spirit.

Her repressed emotions had been wiped away like cleaning a lint trap in a dryer and wiping off the fluff. Deep core states of her being had been transmuted into a finer energy like an alchemist altering the substance of one fine metal into a precious metal.

Her broken and shattered heart and body have begun to mold back together, and the gold adhesive does not hide the scars. Rather, it exposes what she has been through, and she is beginning to see the value in her suffering.

Falling Snow

And now, back to snow and the beauty that is observed when it falls. This woman has found solace in snowfall, which has been present in so many difficult and anguishing moments of her life.

She once wrote these words to me:

> "It's as though God has sent his blanket of peace down to comfort me. The night my son was born, I was at home alone in the bathtub with my shotgun on one side and a bottle of whisky on the other. After he was born, it began to snow. What a beautiful and peaceful sight. The night I buried him I was sitting above the baby cemetery . . . with my shotgun on one side and a bottle of whiskey on the other, and of course a shovel. After I buried him, not more than five minutes later, it began to snow. Huge and beautiful snowflakes. As if God was saying, be still . . . I have your son. The day we buried my dad, it was a beautiful sunny May Saturday. Three minutes after the service ended it began to snow, huge and beautiful snowflakes. As if to say, "It's ok, he is with me now." There are so many more accounts, but these are the ones that stand out to me. In my mind, God has graced me with his presence with snow. That is why I love sharing snowflakes with everyone around me. I see it as God's grace showering down on us. It's not about church and checking the box, but it's all about God's grace. God is the only reason I am alive today. And I am fifty years old, and forty-three years in the bonus, so it's time I take action and make the rest of my years count for *Him* and for my girls."

A Story Big Enough to Live In

I believe that it is important for all of us to form our story and articulate it in a way that offers the truth of what we have been through. Knowing and telling our story helps us grieve and process our emotional experiences. As we attend to the story that is written on our hearts, we are guided to finalize our identity and purpose. We come to know who we are and, in some cases, we discover why we went through what we did.

We then need to transcend our story, to live beyond what we know and how we have come to define ourselves. This is the forever story that emphasizes our true self—who we really are—so that our identity and purpose are more clearly seen. As my late friend Brent Curtis (along with John Eldridge) had stated, every one of us needs "a story big enough to live in" (4).

This woman has come face to face with the story that she wanted to ignore and discard; she wanted to pretend it didn't exist and all of it never happened. She has begun to live and speak out her truth to others. She has found warm and supportive listeners to honor and validate her history and experience. She has also come into who she really is, her true self, beyond the story of her life and all that has happened to her.

She is now who she has always been meant to be. She is her *new self* in Christ, renewed in the spirit of her mind (5) and transformed by the renewing of her mind (6). This has been occasioned by courageously speaking the truth in love (7).

We are to seek truth and then live in truth. The truth for this woman has become known. And her fear and shame have not been the version of disaster that she has surmised.

No matter what was occurring in her life she often said to me, "It's all good," even when it was evidently so far from good. What we know now is that it really is all good. So good.

1. Galatians 5:22–23
2. Psalms 3:3, Hebrew Bible
3. Fear is a Liar

4. The Sacred Romance
5. Ephesians 4:23
6. Romans 12:1–2
7. Ephesians 4:15

11
Much Love to You

The Three Loves

Would you like to know what helped this woman the most? It was love. She felt the opposite of love for so long and had such a strong yearning all this time to be loved. Then others started loving her. She received love, and she learned to love herself. That's it!

I cannot think of any other need for any of us at this time but to love and be loved. And also to know that we *are* love above all else. Love is who we are! It is the defining characteristic of our being. We were made in love, by love, and for love because we are love.

One day in the life of Christ, as recorded in the Gospel, certain religious leaders approached him. A particular expert of the law of Moses asked him which commandment was most important.

The teacher Jesus responded by stating that we are to love the Lord our God with all of our heart, all of our soul, and all of our mind. This is the first and most important command. The second one is very much like the first. We are to love others as we love ourselves. Then Christ asserted that all the law and the writings of the prophets depend on these two commands (1).

So, it is all about love. The only rule is love: to know love and be love and to know we are loved and we are love.

To love God with everything you have and are is to dive into the boundaryless sea of divine compassionate affection. This love is a characteristic of God's being and defines the Creator more than anything else. God is love. The Divine not only **has** love but *is* love, as it is an exhaustive characteristic of the nature of this being.

To love God is really to love back. The love of God flows through all time and space, and beyond the reaches of the known physical universe, yet also exists in complete entirety within you. God is loving you unreservedly in every moment. To love God is to receive this boundaryless benevolence and allow it to course through you with the intensity that this divine quality possesses.

There is no tireless effort of trying our hardest here. There is only love and loving in the oneness of being. We do not perform or do love; we let love be, and then we become love.

And then you are commanded to love yourself. This is often the forgotten love. It is the love that is so disregarded that we often don't hear it or acknowledge it when the above passage is read. We do not frequently enough love ourselves in the way that Christ encouraged us to. Remember, what was mentioned in the above passage is a command, so we are commanded to love ourselves.

We may read the above passage as some dutiful obligation to love God, which seems burdensome or impossible. Then as we skip over the essential commandment of self-love, we run right into trying our hardest and with all of our might to be nice to others. At least we can do that: throw out a few kind behaviors each day, and no one will notice we have little idea what love is.

If we really received divine love for ourselves and then loved ourselves with this great love, we would be full, rich, and powerful. This is because love is the most potent force and the greatest power. To hold this capacity within your being is necessary to not only be filled up with God's amazing love but to also allow it to continue its expression as you love yourself. This self-love is not arrogant or self-serving in a way that diminishes others. It is very personal and quiet, yet strong, and others are enhanced and enlarged in the application of this incredible quality.

With all of this tremendous and inexhaustible love coursing through you, you can then invite others to join this love fest by loving them. If you are so filled up to the brim with ***divine compassion,*** you walk into serendipitous encounters knowing that those are the perfect opportunities to give another person the love that they may desperately need in that moment. Or you simply offer a small, kind gesture without fanfare because that may provide hope when there was no hope at all.

There are two commandments that we are invited to fall into, yet there are three loves. Love God with all that your heart. Love yourself. Love others. This power flows down from the high cathedral of divine affection, the robust and burgeoning heart of All That Is, into a precipitous stream that meanders into your open heart. Then take a look around. Someone else most assuredly needs a boost of that perennial power.

Being Like Narcissus

I have found that there are two kinds of so-called narcissists: the giver and the taker. The taker looks outside of themselves to coerce or manipulate others into providing for them. The giver looks outside of themselves to provide something for others. Both neglect themselves and their own growth by looking outside of themselves to give or take.

In this state, the inner life of the heart is not considered or nurtured at all. The giver and the taker operate in a version of so-called love that is really fear-based and externally preoccupied.

Christ encouraged us to look inside of ourselves to find love. This is a love that is to be received from God and applied liberally to self and others. True love is discovered in us and not in another person or object or activity. It is not necessary to search outside of ourselves for what we already have within.

In Greek mythology, the young man Narcissus stared longingly and fell in love with his own reflection in the waters of a spring until he was no more. What is left of his existence is the flower that bears his name. Perhaps this version of self-love, a focused looking at and within oneself, is what was encouraged by many spiritual masters and traditions through the ages.

It is in this way that dying has a purpose. Death as the dissolution of the ego is to be welcomed on the spiritual path. You know your progress has taken you far when you become a flower. We need more flowers like Narcissus. This would be the best version of advancement: instead of focusing on what is outside, focus on the flowering of the inner self of the heart.

For this woman in our story, her journey into true love has been painful yet also illuminating. She has met many takers, and they sought to extract from her what she concluded she was supposed to give. So she gave, and gave, and gave because her environment and those in it demanded from her.

Now she has learned to not give so much, at least not in that diminishing way. She gives to herself by loving herself with love's power, which originates within her. Then she can give to others by loving them with what she has nurtured within herself. Self-love is the energy behind giving to the other, and *divine love* is the power that enables us to love ourselves in a way that is most enriching and nourishing. Anything else depletes and is an affront to what love really is.

You cannot give away what you don't have. Nurturing something within yourself enables you to build something that can be offered to anyone anywhere. I am so pleased that this woman knows this. She knows love. May we all.

My Story with Love

My wife and I were able to teach our three sons about love. There was a sufficient amount of love flowing in our home so that when our oldest son came home from college with psychotic mental illness, we knew what to do. We loved him. He received our love, and then, most importantly, he loved himself.

Love was the tonic that trickled into the cracks and crevices of a mind that was out of balance to provide a remedy. It was the power that dismantled wayward structures and ushered my son into wholeness and health. He is truly a marvel to this day, a product of the greatest power in the universe. It was love that saved the day and brought my son back to a sound mind.

Our second son was a great lover and still is, although he was transferred from his life on earth to the next domain on December 15, 2012. I still feel his love often. The amount of powerful love we feel from him as a family is remarkable. Isn't it grand that love is stronger than what is known as death? This is because beyond the apparent bounds of time and space, farther than all of the dimensions and densities known to us at this point, or even those not yet known, there is love.

Our youngest son is learning love, particularly self-love with all of its subtle nuances, as it finds its way into and out of his ever-burgeoning heart. Love is healing him from all of his hurts, losses, and disruptions in life. It is becoming his power, an impetus to descend into the finer rhythms of a greater life to a self that is more true.

A Journey of Love

When I met this woman, she had little idea about or experience with love. She received a particular measure of love from her parents and maintained a loving relationship with them over the years, at least to a certain degree.

She had enough love to be a very good mother, loving and protecting her daughters quite fiercely. Her love for her girls was strong, vigilant, and protective.

She had enough of a representation of love to be a loving wife, although remember, this was generated mostly by fear and shame. Her extension of love to her husband was met with hurt, pain, control, rage, and devaluing.

She was a good friend, although she kept others at a distance, and people knew her as kind and helpful. She has now given the nod of approval for others to love her, and she takes it in.

She is finally, once and for all, learning to love herself. Self-love in itself is a healing balm, enriching her so that many areas of her being are being renewed. Love is bringing her into a wholeness she has longed for all of these years, and she can't help but love what and who she is now.

Most of all, she is experiencing divine love, knowing without a shadow of a doubt that God is deeply and unconditionally in love with her. These are the streams flowing in and through her with an impulse that can only originate from the source.

A Positive Impact in our Community

Here is one big way this woman has loved others. She has always had a huge heart for children and adolescents. She had fostered twenty-seven children over a twenty-five-year period. Even more, she worked in our community in places that assured her contact with the youth. She offered tireless and selfless acts of devotion to many young people.

She had so often put herself in a position to be around youth in order to pour love into them so they will feel valued. Even when she was in the midst of her own pain that no one knew about, she gave to others, especially to children and adolescents. This was because she knew that children are vulnerable and could easily be harmed; she provided the care and protection she so desperately wanted for herself. She gave to the youth in our town what precious few, if any, were willing to give to her.

In a way, she bypassed her own pain in order to alleviate the suffering of others. It may have been a distraction so she wouldn't have to focus on her own decimated heart. Nonetheless, many of the young were the recipients of her kindness.

A Love for All

There is something this woman and I want you to know. We would like for you to experience this love above all else, no matter what conditions define your life.

It is our hope that you come into a love from God or Christ or Source or All That Is or Self, or whatever you know this power as. We long for you to love yourself with a robust enough love to sustain you in all your days. We wish, too, that there would be someone around who can express strong love to you and that you would receive it willingly.

There is a video that I have found helpful through the years. I have played this video several times for this woman. The song "Oh How He Loves Us" is by Kim Walker-Smith. The link is here: https://www.youtube.com/watch?v=JoC1ec-lYps. Please enjoy, and

"You better just brace yourself!"

I wrote the poem below, and it is published in the book *A Present Moment Embrace: The Breath within the Breath and the Music between the Notes.* The poem is called "The Most Essential Thing" and is included here in its entirety:

> "The most powerful and essential teaching
>   Is always Love
> Love is our foundation and core
>   It is our destiny and purpose.
>
> It is where we come from as Original Cause
>   And what we are moving toward
> In the broad endless reach
>   Of Infinity's unlimited dimensions.
>
> When faith and hope and love are evident
> As the finest qualities of human experience
>   The greatest of these is always love.
>
> We all need to clear away the impediments
> That prohibit the expression
> Of receiving and participating in
>   The foundation of love
> And there is no other quality greater
>   Than love.
>
> God's love is planted inside each of us by Spirit
> In the deepest depths of the human heart
>   And inner consciousness
> It is Spirit who waters and causes growth
> And then provides the impetus
> For love to flow out of us
>   In torrential flow.
>
> Then it is realized at long last
>   That love is who you are

In the True Self of eternal spirit
> As it always has been.

When you are not living in reference to love
You are outside the borders of pure simple being
> Being untrue to your essential Divine nature.

Yet when love is the expression
You are representing the dignity of the Imago Dei
The true being from Eternity's endless reach
> Positioned conveniently in your very Center.

We are to remind ourselves each day
> Of what we have known since the Origins
It is what your True Self knows, and is
> As you reconnect yourself to Source.

The Holy Trinity, as the mystery beyond mysteries
> Is deeply in love with itself
And this Divine Love flows incessantly
In and through and between these dynamic personalities
And we are to meander within this creative impulse
> As we mirror the Creator in who and what It is.

We are created by a loving God
> And are called to be love
In the ordinary contexts of our lives
> In every day and moment that we have to live.

Love helps us realize that there is no separateness
> In love we are all one, every one of us
In the cryptic pouring forth of love's Divine impulse
> We engage in a union with anyone and everyone.

For, in truth, we are love, and we are one . . . always
> And always have been

> From eternity forward and backward
> To the present time" (2).

I hope this has expressed the power of love in all of its fine reverberations and unremitting pulsations. And as we end this chapter, I have something to tell you. I love you.

And out of the deep love in her heart, this woman wants to express her love to you as well. She is sending her love because she has been in the place where love did not seem to be present at all. There was no love to apprehend or hold onto when she needed it the most. There was no love to soothe her aching heart and fill her in a way that she so desperately craved.

She has it now, and it is the love she longs to send to you, particularly if you are in the same place that she was in before.

> If you are empty and alone, know you are loved.
> If you are being abused or devalued, know you are loved.
> If someone is hurting you in any way, know you are loved.
> If you have yet to realize your worth and value, know you are loved.
> If you have disappointment and your hope has been dashed, know you are loved.
> If you desire connection with others or someone and have yet to find the bonding your heart and body aches for, know you are loved.
> If life has assaulted you and been unkind, know you are loved.
> If you are in grief or sorrow for a loss you cannot imagine overcoming, know you are loved.
> If you don't see any purpose for your life and are contemplating ending your life, please know you are loved.
> If your fears, anxiety, sadness, or any other emotion is so strong and overwhelming that you feel like you are drowning, know you are loved.

If you have anguish and your despair has drained you of peace and comfort, know you are loved.

Know, dear friend, whoever you are, that you are so very loved.

1. Matthew 22:34–40; NIV
2. "A Present Moment Embrace" by Tom Steward

Afterword

No Grave Can Hold You Down

    This woman and I were talking recently, and she told me about a song she heard that she really liked. I looked it up, and we played it while we sat in my office. It is performed by Johnny Cash and is entitled "Ain't No Grave." Here are the lyrics:

> There ain't no grave can hold my body down
> There ain't no grave can hold my body down
> When I hear that trumpet sound I'm gonna rise right out of the ground
> Ain't no grave can hold my body down
>
> Well, look way down the river, what do you think I see?
> I see a band of angels and they're coming after me
> Ain't no grave can hold my body down
> There ain't no grave can hold my body down
>
> Well, look down yonder Gabriel, put your feet on the land and see
> But Gabriel don't you blow your trumpet 'til you hear it from me
> There ain't no grave can hold my body down
> Ain't no grave can hold my body down

Well, meet me Jesus, meet me. Meet me in the middle of
the air
And if these wings don't fail me, I will meet you anywhere
Ain't no grave can hold my body down
There ain't no grave can hold my body down

Well, meet me mother and father, meet me down the river
road
And momma you know that I'll be there when I check in
my load
Ain't no grave can hold my body down
There ain't no grave can hold my body down
There ain't no grave can hold my body down

It's true. No grave can hold anyone down. A grave or wooden box or an urn of ashes is a receptacle meant to hold the physical remains of the body we had on earth. We are not that body. We are spirit, one with All That Is. Always have been and always will be.

Not only that, but no life circumstance, person, long season of pain, or even a life of turmoil and abuse will be able to hold us down. When we are knocked down, we get up. We must get up. We must overcome. Nothing is meant to defeat us. Everything we go through strengthens us, even though this is so difficult to see while we are in a skirmish with adversity.

Halloween, the Transfer Date

Each year, Halloween comes and goes, and most people view it as a time of fun and gathering. Not for this woman. It's the anniversary date of Timmy's murder.

This year, I sent her this text:

> "Many blessings to you this day, dear friend. In remembrance of the beautiful eternal soul known here as Timmy, whose transcendent essence resides with Christ's divine spirit of love in the heavenly realms. May he touch you, his mama, today even more than all of the other

days. May he and the Spirit mend your heart completely and lift it up high. May the radiant light of eternity shine upon you and give you peace. May you know contentment and gratitude and love this day, the one day. Love to you."

No grave has held Timmy down either. He lived here for a short time yet lives on elsewhere for a very long endless time. His life, sad and tragic as it was, is a reminder that what is here is important, yet it is only a small part of the full depth and breadth of the expansive timelessness we are often not conscious of enough.

The Life That Has Been Chosen

I often wonder why people go through what they do. I ponder why there is so much suffering and evil in this world we live in. Our inhumanity to each other is anguishing and, in some cases, pulverizing. So many have been torn asunder in body, soul, and spirit. There are times I can hardly stand up under the truth of it all when I hear the stories of those who are recipients of the unconscionable behavior of another.

Is there some sort of design or purpose behind it all? Did we choose beforehand the life that we are living because we knew it was critical for the evolution of our soul? If so, how we proceed through our struggles is vital as we learn and grow through these well-choreographed and previously concocted lessons.

No one is a victim. We are all survivors in some way. In some cases, we may see how we are victors, victorious over the roadblocks and challenges that have been placed before us.

This is true for all of us. We are here for a purpose. Our lives are important, and each one of us has immense value and worth.

We have help as there are those in a world nearby who look upon us and see our plight. They see who we are, and they guide us more than we know.

It truly is about so much more than the physical realm that appears to be ever so present. We are spirits from another place who inhabit a body for a short time for a purpose, and we have to get to the end, and to end well, as we transcend our mortal experience and realize there is so much more. And we, yes, every one of us, are an important part of that "more."

I hope reading and telling this woman's story has been a reminder to you of the high stakes inherent in the lives we are living. Just so you know, she continues to do well and is living a triumphant life beyond all odds. She is a marvel, a lovely soul, and a dear friend.

Many blessings to you this day and all days, in tribute to that one day of eternity.

Love to you, beloved.

Lightning Source UK Ltd.
Milton Keynes UK
UKHW011836161222
414070UK00012B/367/J

9 781664 167544